# DAY HIKES ON

# Kauai

## 55 GREAT HIKES

### Robert Stone

3rd EDITION

**Day Hike Books, Inc.**

RED LODGE, MONTANA

Published by Day Hike Books, Inc.
P.O. Box 865
Red Lodge, Montana 59068

Distributed by The Globe Pequot Press
246 Goose Lane
P.O. Box 480
Guilford, CT 06437-0480
800-243-0495 (direct order) · 800-820-2329 (fax order)
www.globe-pequot.com

Photographs by Robert Stone
Design by Paula Doherty

The author has made every attempt to provide accurate information in this book. However, trail routes and features may change—please use common sense and forethought, and be mindful of your own capabilities. Let this book guide you, but be aware that each hiker assumes responsibility for their own safety. The author and publisher do not assume any responsibility for loss, damage or injury caused through the use of this book.

Cover photo: Wailua Falls, Hike 22
Back cover photo: Waimea Canyon, page 14

# Table of Contents

## THE HIKES

### Waimea Canyon and
### Kokee State Park

## The South Coast

## Wailua River watershed

# The North Coast

# About the Hikes

Some of the finest hikes in all Hawaii and possibly the world are found on the island of Kauai. From precarious cliffs to relaxing strolls through botanical gardens, these 55 day hikes offer the hiker excellent possibilities to explore and enrich their time spent on Kauai.

All levels of hiking experience are accommodated in this guide, with an emphasis on outstanding scenery and memorable features. Each hike includes a map, detailed driving and hiking directions and a summary. An overall map of Kauai and the locations of hikes is found on pages 10-11.

The verdant "Garden Isle" of Kauai is an emerald green gem of lush foliage, cascading waterfalls, dramatic valleys and canyons. The 553-square-mile island of Kauai is Hawaii's oldest and northernmost island. Mount Waialeale, the wettest place on earth, averages 451 inches of rain annually. It is the source of Kauai's seven major rivers and many of its waterfalls. Nearly half of the 335,000-acre island is mountainous forest, accessible only by its hiking trails.

To help you decide which hikes are most appealing to you, a brief summary of the highlights is included with each hike. You may enjoy these areas for a short time or the whole day. Reference the overall map to locate the general location of the hikes.

Polihale State Park is a two-mile strip of sandy beach on the dry west coast of Kauai. The park's sheer, majestic grey cliffs and jagged peaks rise above the wide stretch of white sand and the deep blue ocean beyond. The park has picnic facilities and is an ideal spot for viewing sunsets. Hike 1 is a beach stroll through this state park.

The colossal Waimea Canyon, known as the Grand Canyon of the Pacific, is ten miles in length with glowing jewel-colored cathedral walls that descend 3,000 feet. The cool, wet high country of Kokee State Park, adjacent to Waimea Canyon, is a lush 4,300-acre wilderness preserve with more than 40 miles of hiking trails and freshwater streams. The trails wind through the forest and along the canyon rim. There are 14 hikes found in the canyon and Kokee area (see page 14).

Along the dry, sunny south coast of Kauai are the white sand beaches of Poipu—Hikes 18-20. These beaches are an excellent place to spend the day beachcombing, exploring tidepools and promontories, and enjoying the water. Pools, blowholes, off-shore reefs and coves are here to discover from either land or water.

The Wailua River watershed flows through a lush valley to the island's east coast. Beautiful forests and waterfalls are highlights for the 13 hikes that lie throughout the valley. Wailua Falls (cover photo) and Opaekaa Falls are two of the lovelier waterfalls. For a magnificent hike to the interior of the island, try the Powerline Trail.

Along the tropical north shore are quaint one-lane bridges, rainbows and serene villages with weathered houses, flowering gardens and overgrown hedges of hibiscus and plumeria. Crescent-shaped beaches lie nestled between tall sea cliffs and waterfalls drop into picture-perfect. (See the north coast hikes, page 82). On the northernmost point of Kauai is the 52-foot Kilauea Lighthouse, built in 1913 and now within the Kilauea National Wildlife Refuge. The lighthouse sits on a peninsula that offers a great vantage point for observing birds, seals, dolphins, sea turtles and humpback whales.

Na Pali State Park on the northwest coast of Kauai is home to the awesome Na Pali coastline, with primeval emerald green valleys and imposing perpendicular cliffs plunging 4,000 feet to the cobalt blue Pacific. The state park, which takes in 6,000 acres, is accessible only by foot or boat. The Kalalau Trail hugs the coastline while winding along these cliffs in Kalalau Valley (Hikes 54 and 55).

If you have little time to hike but still want to enjoy a few trails, try the Pihea Trail (Hike 2), the scalloped beaches on the south coast (Hikes 18, 19 and 20) and the Kalalau Trail along the Na Pali Coast (Hikes 54 and 55). These hikes offer some of the most beautiful and incredible scenery found in Kauai.

Getting around Kauai is easy. All of the hikes are accessed via the main highway that lies along the perimeter of the island— Highway 50 or Highway 56, depending on your direction out of Lihue. The highway markers roughly correspond with mileage distances in each direction beginning in Lihue at mile marker "0." The Waimea Canyon/Kokee trailheads are right off Kokee Road, the main access road for the parks. All of the hikes are an hour's drive or less from anywhere on the island. Be cautious, however, of unpaved roads. Their conditions can change rapidly because of frequent rainfalls.

Be prepared with appropriate hiking attire and a few necessities. Wear supportive, comfortable hiking shoes that won't mind getting a little muddy. Wet rain forests to dry deserts will make it necessary to have a variety of clothing when exploring Kauai. Be sure to bring a hat and rain jacket. Sunscreen, inset repellent, sunglasses, drinking water and snacks are a must. Don't forget swimwear and outdoor gear to use at the coast.

Enjoy the trails and scenery! Your day will be enhanced with a hike in Kauai's beautiful landscape.

# Waimea Canyon and Kokee State Park

Waimea Canyon and the Kokee State Park area are referred to as the "Grand Canyon of the Pacific." The canyon measures ten miles long by one mile wide, with a depth of 3,000 feet (photo on back cover). Sheer cliffs and multicolored canyon walls with cascading waterfalls are typical views. The Kokee area adjacent to the canyon includes everything from high mountain peaks that overlook the sea to atmospheric swampy landscapes dripping with lush vegetation.

Hikes 2-15 explore this exquisite area of the island. These 14 hikes, which include 50 miles of trails, offer an excellent cross-section of all that these state parks have to offer. The views into this ancient and richly colored canyon highlight the layers of black, red, purple and pink rock framed by the changing cloud formations. These selected hikes have a variety of scenic overlooks into the canyon, deep jungle trails with lush vegetation, streams, waterfalls and swimming pools. Wild pigs and goats may be spotted on any of the hikes.

Kokee State Park, north of Waimea Canyon, lies on a cool plateau with quiet forests and excellent vantage points for viewing the northwest coast from afar. Trails lead through thick, shady jungles teeming with the songs of birds. The area has a lodge with cabin rentals and a restaurant. Next to the lodge is the Kokee Natural History Museum, a superb facility offering everything you would want to know about the area, plus a gift shop with books and maps.

A map of the canyon and park is found on pages 14-15.

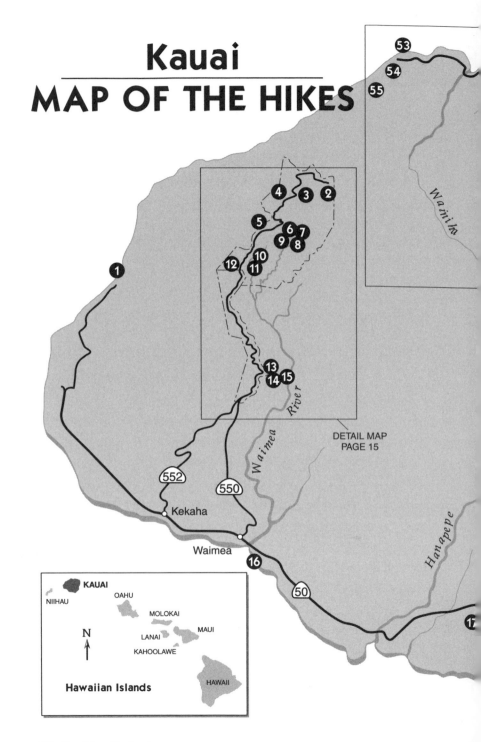

# Kauai
# MAP OF THE HIKES

DETAIL MAP
PAGE 15

Wainiha

Waimea River

552

550

Kekaha

Waimea

50

Hanapepe

KAUAI

NIIHAU

OAHU

MOLOKAI

LANAI

MAUI

KAHOOLAWE

HAWAII

N

Hawaiian Islands

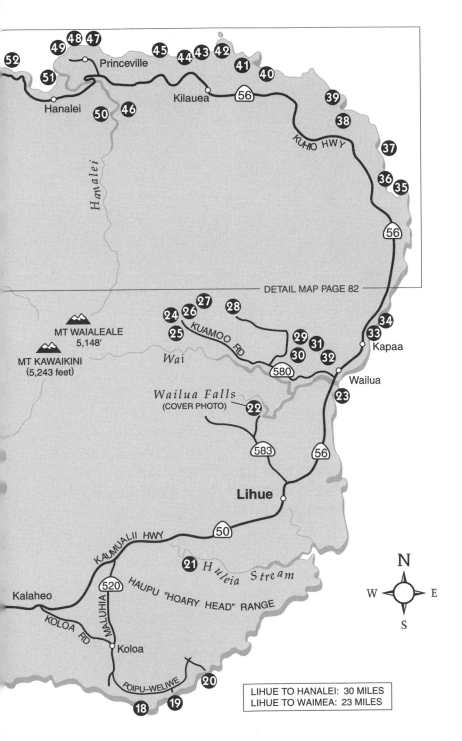

Princeville

Kilauea

KUHIO HWY

Hanalei

DETAIL MAP PAGE 82

MT WAIALEALE
5,148'

MT KAWAIKINI
(5,243 feet)

Wai

KUAMOO RD

Kapaa

Wailua

Wailua Falls
(COVER PHOTO)

Lihue

KAUMUALII HWY

Huleia Stream

Kalaheo

HAUPU "HOARY HEAD" RANGE

MALUHIA

KOLOA RD

Koloa

POIPU–WELIWE

N
W — E
S

LIHUE TO HANALEI: 30 MILES
LIHUE TO WAIMEA: 23 MILES

# Hike 1
## Polihale State Park and Beach

**Hiking distance:** 0.5 to 4 miles round trip
**Hiking time:** 1 to 3 hours
**Elevation gain:** Level
**Maps:** U.S.G.S. Makaha Point
Earthwalk Press Northwestern Kauai Recreation Map

**Summary of hike:** Polihale State Park is a remote 140-acre park at the end of the road on the western end of Kauai. The park offers access to 15 miles of uninterrupted sand beach from Polihale Ridge, at the southwest end of the Na Pali cliffs, to Kekaha Beach Park. This hike follows the long sandy strand from the base of the spectacular Na Pali peaks to Barking Sands Beach by the Pacific Missile Range Facility. The islands of Niihau and Lehua are visible across the channel. Facilities include restrooms, showers, picnic shelters and campsites.

**Driving directions:** From Lihue, drive 39 miles west on Highway 50 to the end of the highway, seven miles past the town of Kekaha. Shortly after the Pacific Missile Range Facility, the road forks. Take the fork to the right (east) for 0.5 miles to the first left turn. Turn left, as the sign directs, onto a cane field road. Continue 1.8 miles to the end of the road and turn left. Drive toward the ocean 3.1 miles to the Polihale day use parking area. Turn left and park.

**Hiking directions:** From the parking area, walk towards the ocean. Begin to the right, exploring the forbidding, vertical Na Pali cliffs. On the slopes, hidden in the brush at the edge of the cliffs, are the remains of an ancient *heiau* (temple). Now head left on the long expanse of isolated beach that stretches for miles. The back end of the beach is bordered by massive dunes, reaching as high as 100 feet at Nohili Point. Follow the coastline southwest towards Barking Sands Beach and the sand dunes. The Pacific Missile Range Facility is two miles down the beach, which you cannot miss. It is a good turnaround spot.

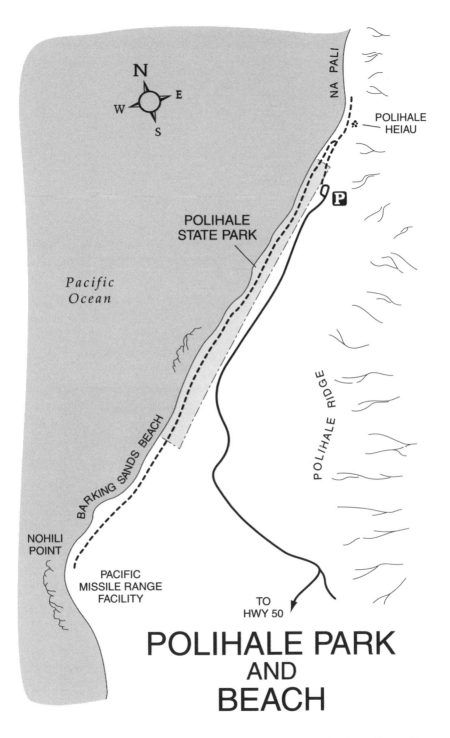

N
W E
S

NA PALI

POLIHALE
HEIAU

**P**

POLIHALE
STATE PARK

*Pacific
Ocean*

POLIHALE RIDGE

BARKING SANDS BEACH

NOHILI
POINT

PACIFIC
MISSILE RANGE
FACILITY

TO
HWY 50

# POLIHALE PARK
## AND
# BEACH

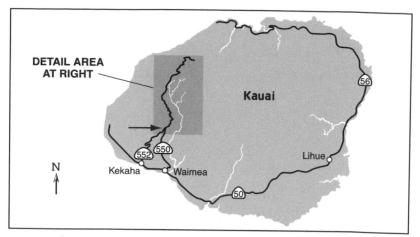

# Waimea Canyon and Kokee State Park
# Hikes 2-15

Driving directions for hikes 2 through 15 begin from the junction in Waimea Canyon where Waimea Canyon Drive/Highway 550 and Kokee Road/Highway 552 merge (indicated by the arrow). To arrive at this junction, follow these directions:

### FROM LIHUE, TWO ROUTES LEAD TO THIS JUNCTION:

**ROUTE 1.** Drive 23 miles southwest on Highway 50 to Waimea Canyon Drive/Highway 550 in the town of Waimea, just beyond mile marker 23. Turn right and drive 6.7 miles to the junction where the road merges with Kokee Road/Highway 552.

**ROUTE 2.** Drive 26.5 miles southwest on Highway 50 to Alae Road (which becomes Kokee Road/Highway 552) in the town of Kekaha. The well-signed turnoff is between mile markers 26 and 27. Turn right and drive 7.6 miles to the junction where the road merges with Waimea Canyon Drive/Highway 550.

Due to the frequency of rain in this area, it is not advisable to drive on unpaved roads with two-wheel drive vehicles. Doing so could lead to a "day hike" back to civilization. Check with the Kokee Lodge or the Kokee Natural History Museum to find out current road conditions.

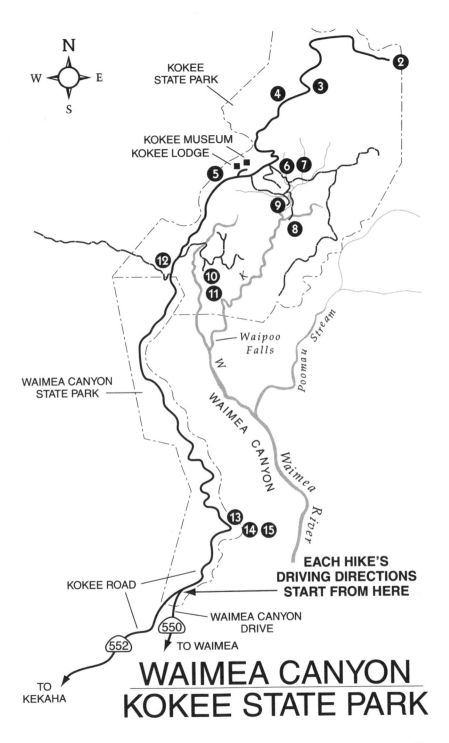

N

W — E

S

KOKEE
STATE PARK

2

4  3

KOKEE MUSEUM
KOKEE LODGE

5  6 7

9

8

12

10
11

K

*Waipoo Falls*

*Poomau Stream*

WAIMEA CANYON
STATE PARK

W

*WAIMEA CANYON*

*Waimea River*

13

14  15

**EACH HIKE'S
DRIVING DIRECTIONS
START FROM HERE**

KOKEE ROAD

550
WAIMEA CANYON
DRIVE

552

TO WAIMEA

TO
KEKAHA

# WAIMEA CANYON
# KOKEE STATE PARK

# Hike 2
# Pihea Trail

**Hiking distance:** 3.5 miles round trip
**Hiking time:** 2 hours
**Elevation gain:** 450 feet
**Maps:** U.S.G.S. Haena
Trails of Kokee State Park map
Earthwalk Press Northwestern Kauai Recreation Map

**Summary of hike:** The Pihea Trail is among the premier hiking paths in the Kokee/Waimea Canyon area. The trail traverses the narrow ridge in the Na Pali Kona Forest Reserve between the Kalalau Valley, the largest valley along the Na Pali cliffs, and the Alakai Swamp. The views extend 4,000 feet down the mossy, fluted cliffs of the Kalalau Valley, which drops sharply into the ocean. The views inland extend over layers of folded forested canyons and ridges to Mount Waialeale, the wettest spot on earth with an average of 451 inches of annual rainfall. Alakai Swamp is an incredible, atmospheric area like nowhere else.

**Driving directions:** From the junction of Waimea Canyon Drive and Kokee Road in Waimea Canyon (directions to junction on page 14) drive 8.7 miles up the winding canyon to the Kokee Lodge and museum on the left. Continue 3.8 miles past the museum turnoff to the Pihea Trail parking lot at the road's end.

**Hiking directions:** Take the paved path a short distance to the 4,280-foot Puu O Kila Lookout. After marveling at the views, follow the edge of the cliffs downhill on the wet eroded path, crossing large red rock slabs. The path is usually muddy and slippery. Continue over numerous rises, dips and several short boardwalks along the rim of the Kalalau Valley. The panoramic, everchanging views are stunning. At 1.1 mile, the path reaches a junction near Pihea Peak. The short, steep spur trail veers left to Pihea Vista. Continue on the main trail, leaving the rim of Kalalau Valley. Descend southeast, skirting the bogs into the forbidding Alakai Swamp, a very large bog at the foot of

Mount Waialeale. Boardwalks allow easy access into the swampy atmosphere. At 1.75 miles, the trail intersects the Alakai Swamp Trail. This is our turnaround spot.

To hike further, both the Pihea Trail and the Alakai Swamp Trail continue downhill to Mohihi Road at 3.7 miles.

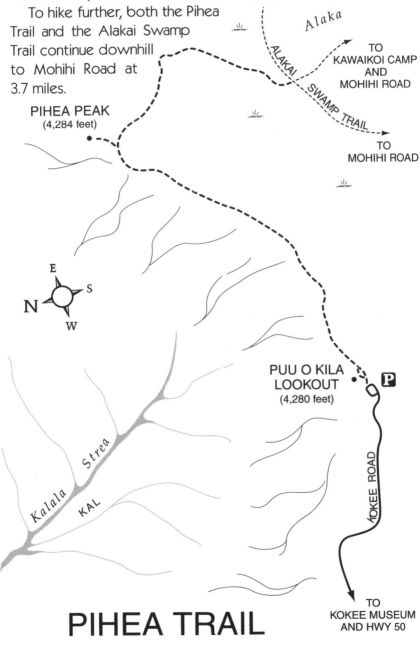

TO KAWAIKOI CAMP AND MOHIHI ROAD

TO MOHIHI ROAD

PIHEA PEAK
(4,284 feet)

ALAKAI SWAMP TRAIL

Alaka

PUU O KILA LOOKOUT
(4,280 feet)

P

KOKEE ROAD

Kalala Strea

KAL

TO KOKEE MUSEUM AND HWY 50

# PIHEA TRAIL

# Hike 3
# Kaluapuhi Trail to Kalalau Lookout

**Hiking distance:** 3.2 miles round trip
**Hiking time:** 1.5 hours
**Elevation gain:** 150 feet
**Maps:** U.S.G.S. Haena
Trails of Kokee State Park

**Summary of hike:** The Kaluapuhi Trail (also called the Plum Grove Trail) follows a wide, flat grassy path through a beautiful forest of ohia, guava, plum, ginger and blackberries. The trail travels through the intimate surroundings of a pastoral garden on its way to Kalalau Lookout, a 4,000-foot vista point. The panoramic views from the lookout extend down the fluted green cliffs and knife-edged ridges of the Kalalau Valley to the Na Pali coastline.

**Driving directions:** From the junction of Waimea Canyon Drive and Kokee Road in Waimea Canyon (directions to junction on page 14) drive 8.7 miles up the winding canyon to the Kokee Lodge and museum on the left. Continue 1.6 miles past the museum turnoff to the Awaawapuhi Trail parking lot on the left. It is located just beyond mile marker 17. Turn left and park.

**Hiking directions:** Head northeast on Kokee Road for 0.3 miles, reaching the Kaluapuhi Trail on the right. Climb a short grassy hill and head east along the level, forested path. A half mile along the path is a T-junction. The right fork fades into the brush. Take the left fork and head north to Kokee Road. Walk 0.2 miles left (west) along the road to a paved pullout and footpath on the right. Take the forested path a short distance to a grassy flat and picnic area. Beyond the flat is Kalalau Lookout perched on the cliff's edge, offering fantastic views down the Kalalau Valley. Return along the same route.

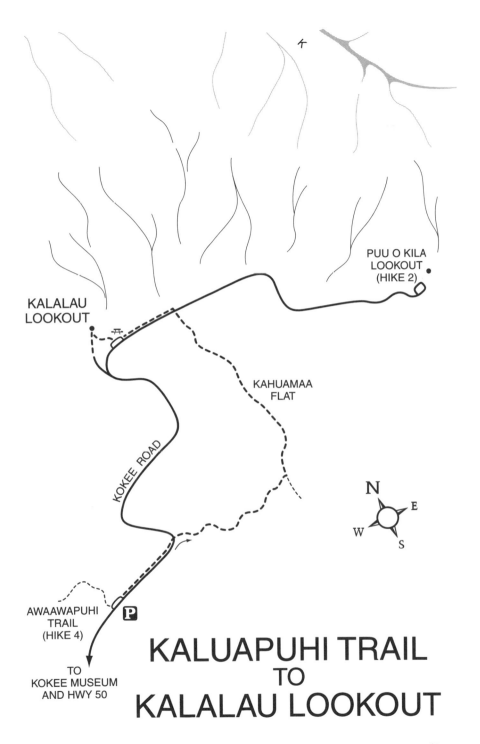

PUU O KILA
LOOKOUT
(HIKE 2)

KALALAU
LOOKOUT

KAHUAMAA
FLAT

KOKEE ROAD

N
W E
S

AWAAWAPUHI
TRAIL
(HIKE 4)

TO
KOKEE MUSEUM
AND HWY 50

# KALUAPUHI TRAIL
## TO
# KALALAU LOOKOUT

# Hike 4
# Awaawapuhi Trail

**Hiking distance:** 6.5 miles round trip
**Hiking time:** 3.5 hours
**Elevation gain:** 1,600 feet
**Maps:** U.S.G.S. Haena and Makaha Point
      Trails of Kokee State Park

**Summary of hike:** This hike descends to the edge of the sheer cliffs and razor-edged ridges of the Nualolo and Awaawapuhi Valleys. There are inspiring panoramas of the steep, 3000-foot vertical cliffs to the isolated Na Pali coast, accessible only by water. This trail can be combined with the Nualolo Trail (Hike 5) for a 9-mile loop hike. The two trails are connected by the Nualolo Cliffs Trail, a 2.2 mile connector trail that follows the rim of Nualolo Valley.

**Driving directions:** From the junction of Waimea Canyon Drive and Kokee Road in Waimea Canyon (directions to junction on page 14) drive 8.7 miles up the winding canyon to the Kokee Lodge and museum on the left. Continue 1.6 miles past the museum turnoff to the Awaawapuhi Trail parking lot on the left. It is located just beyond mile marker 17. Turn left and park.

**Hiking directions:** The trail begins on the south side of the parking lot and immediately enters the shade of the forest canopy. At a half mile, switchbacks descend through a lush, humid forest. Endemic trees and bushes are labeled along the way. At just under 2 miles, views open to the steep forested cliffs of the Awaawapuhi and Nualolo Valleys. There are several lookouts along the trail. At 3 miles is a junction with the Nualolo Cliffs Trail on the left. If you plan to return on the same path, stay to the right and continue on the Awaawapuhi Trail. In a quarter mile, the trail terminates at a metal railing, perched on the precarious ridge dividing the Awaawapuhi and Nualolo Valleys. The views extend from the steep, eroded cliffs 2,500 feet down to the ocean. Return by retracing your steps.

To hike the 9-mile loop, take the near-level Nualolo Cliffs Trail along the rim of the Na Pali cliffs for two miles to the Nualolo Trail (Hike 5).

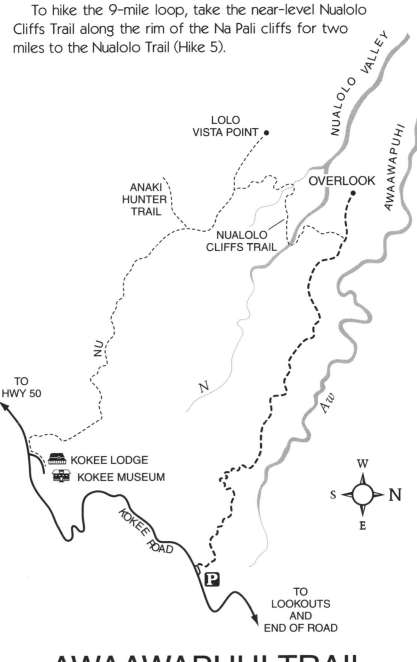

# AWAAWAPUHI TRAIL

# Hike 5
# Nualolo Trail

**Hiking distance:** 7.5 miles round trip
**Hiking time:** 4 hours
**Elevation gain:** 1,600 feet
**Maps:** U.S.G.S. Haena and Makaha Point
   Trails of Kokee State Park

**Summary of hike:** This hike descends through a lush forest to panoramic vistas of the Na Pali coastline. The trail ends at Lolo Vista Point, a vertical perch 3,000 feet above the windswept cliffs of the Nualolo Valley. (If it is raining, this trail is not recommended, as several steep sections are dangerous.) This hike can be combined with the Awaawapuhi Trail (Hike 4) for a 9-mile loop hike. The two trails are connected by the Nualolo Cliffs Trail, a 2.2 mile connector trail with phenomenal views of the Na Pali coast. The Cliff Trail follows the rim's edge at the head of the Nualolo Valley, 3,000 feet above the ocean.

**Driving directions:** From the junction of Waimea Canyon Drive and Kokee Road in Waimea Canyon (directions to junction on page 14) drive 8.7 miles up the winding canyon to the Kokee Lodge and museum on the left. Turn left and park in the lot by the museum.

**Hiking directions:** Walk back down Kokee Road 50 yards to the signed trail on the right. Follow the trail sign a few yards to the right, reaching a signed footpath on the left. Short, steep switchbacks contour along the forested hillside. Cross over Kaunuohua Ridge, entering the Kuia Natural Area Reserve at 0.2 miles. Descend northwest through the dense forest for several miles. At 3 miles is a trail split. The Anaki Hunter Route bears left. Stay to the right, and steeply descend to a signed junction with the Nualolo Cliffs Trail at 3.4 miles. If you plan to return on the same path, stay to the left and continue on the Nualolo Trail. The trail follows the southwest rim of the Nualolo Valley on an eroded slope. Pass numerous panoramic vistas to Lolo Vista

Point overlooking the dramatic valley.

To hike the 9-mile loop, take the near-level Nualolo Cliffs Trail along the rim of the Na Pali cliffs for two miles to a T-junction with the Awaawapuhi Trail (Hike 4).

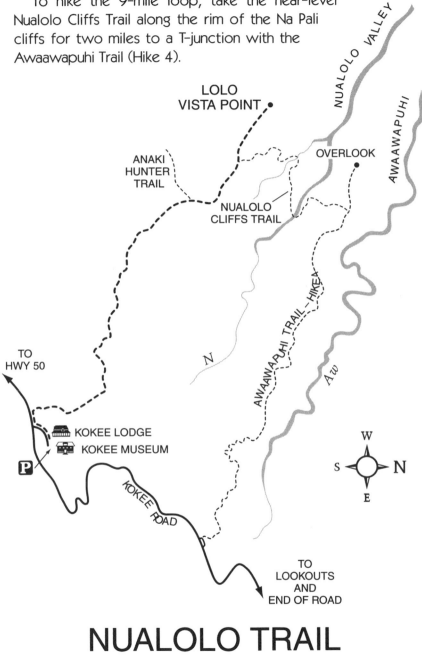

# NUALOLO TRAIL

# Hike 6
# Puu Ka Ohelo—Water Tank Loop

**Hiking distance:** 2.2 mile loop
**Hiking time:** 1 hour
**Elevation gain:** 200 feet
**Maps:** U.S.G.S. Haena
Trails of Kokee State Park

**Summary of hike:** This loop hike begins in the shade of the forested Mohihi Road. The trails cross streams and wind through a lush forest, where there is a wild profusion of trees, tropical plants, flowers and berries. The trail passes large koa trees and skirts around and under the long stilted legs of ohia trees.

**Driving directions:** From the junction of Waimea Canyon Drive and Kokee Road in Waimea Canyon (directions to junction on page 14) drive 8.7 miles up the winding canyon to the Kokee Lodge and museum on the left. Continue 0.3 miles past the museum turnoff to the Kokee Campground on the left. Turn left and park in the spaces on the left.

**Hiking directions:** Return to the Kokee Road, and bear left 15 yards to the signed Mohihi Road on the right. Take the unpaved road to an immediate road split. Head left down the forested road. Cross over Noe Stream to a T-junction at 0.4 miles. Bear left, crossing over Elekeniiki Stream to a Y-junction at 0.7 miles. Take the left fork onto the Puu Ka Ohelo Trail, and head gently uphill. The trail levels off and crosses a few down trees to a signed junction. The right fork is the Berry Flat Trail (Hike 7). Take the Water Tank Trail to the left past the "Discovery Center" sign. Head uphill past ohia trees suspended in the air by long, exposed tree roots, traveling through the long legs of one tree. Traverse the hillside, and curve sharply to the left around the headwaters of Elekeniiki Stream. Follow the contours of the hill past a home. The footpath ends at the Kokee Discovery Center Road. Head right for 100 yards to Kokee Road. Go left 0.2 miles to complete the loop at the campground.

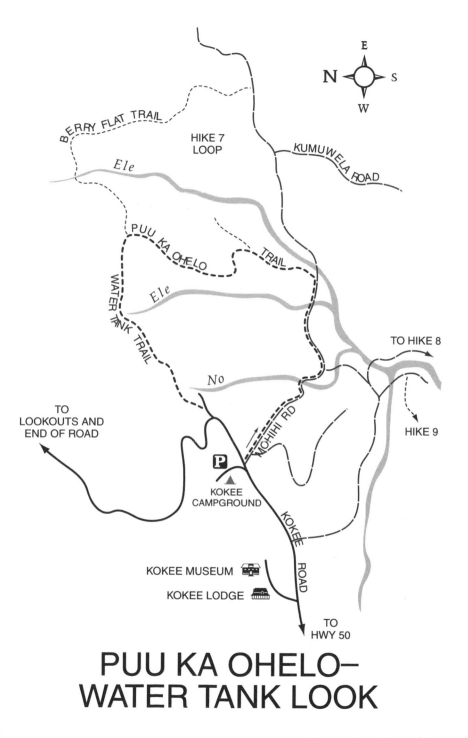

BERRY FLAT TRAIL

HIKE 7 LOOP

KUMUWELA ROAD

N E S W

Ele

PUU KA OHELO

TRAIL

WATER TANK TRAIL

Ele

No

TO HIKE 8

TO LOOKOUTS AND END OF ROAD

HIKE 9

MOHIHI RD

P

KOKEE CAMPGROUND

KOKEE ROAD

KOKEE MUSEUM

KOKEE LODGE

TO HWY 50

# PUU KA OHELO–
# WATER TANK LOOK

# Hike 7
## Puu Ka Ohelo—Berry Flat Loop

**Hiking distance:** 3.4 miles round trip
**Hiking time:** 1.5 hours
**Elevation gain:** 250 feet
**Maps:** U.S.G.S. Haena
Trails of Kokee State Park

**Summary of hike:** This loop hike winds through a dense, tropical jungle with large sugi pine groves and huge California redwoods that were planted in the 1930s. The picturesque jungle is profuse with plants, including red wavy grained koa, eucalyptus trees, strawberry guava trees, ginger, blackberries and long rope-like vines.

**Driving directions:** From the junction of Waimea Canyon Drive and Kokee Road in Waimea Canyon (directions to junction on page 14) drive 8.7 miles up the winding canyon to the Kokee Lodge and museum on the left. Continue 0.3 miles past the museum turnoff to the Kokee Campground on the left. Turn left and park in the spaces on the left.

**Hiking directions:** Return to the Kokee Road, and walk 15 yards left to the signed Mohihi Road on the right. Take the unpaved road, immediately reaching a road fork. Bear left downhill on the forested road, crossing over Noe Stream to a T-junction at 0.4 miles. Bear left and cross over Elekeniiki Stream to a Y-fork at 0.7 miles. Begin the loop to the left on the Puu Ka Ohelo Trail. Head gradually uphill through the forest. Soon the trail levels off and winds through the shady forest canopy, crossing a few fallen trees to a signed junction. The Water Tank Trail (Hike 6) bears left. Go right on the Berry Flat Trail. Wind through the lush forest, crossing the muddy headwaters of Elekeninui Stream. The footpath exits on Mohihi Road. Take the road to the right for a half mile, completing the loop. (Along the way, curve to the right at a road fork with the Kumuwela Road.) Return on the Mohihi Road to the campground.

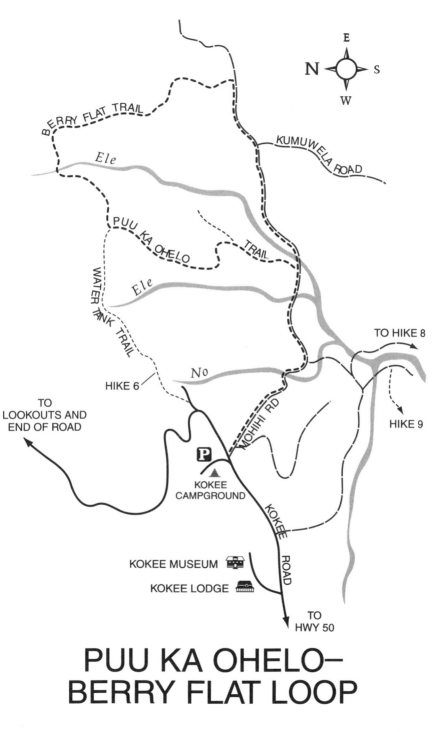

# PUU KA OHELO–
# BERRY FLAT LOOP

# Hike 8
# Kumuwela Trail to Viewpoint

**Hiking distance:** 3 miles round trip
**Hiking time:** 1.5 hours
**Elevation gain:** 350 feet
**Maps:** U.S.G.S. Haena and Waimea Canyon
Trails of Kokee State Park

**Summary of hike:** This is a true jungle hike through a gulch lined with a wild profusion of trees, vines, flowers, tropical plants and massive ferns. You will feel dwarfed by the dense, towering vegetation and vines, which almost smother the massive trees. At the end of the hike are views into Waimea Canyon and the ocean. The trail can be used as an access route for the Black Pipe Trail (Hike 10) and Canyon Trail (Hike 11).

**Driving directions:** From the junction of Waimea Canyon Drive and Kokee Road in Waimea Canyon (directions to junction on page 14) drive 8.7 miles up the winding canyon to the Kokee Lodge and museum on the left. Continue 0.1 mile past the museum turnoff to Kumuwela Road, the first turnoff on the right after the lodge. (The road may be listed as Waineke Road on some maps.) Turn right and drive 0.5 miles to the posted "Camp Sloggett" turnoff on the right. Park at this junction.

**Hiking directions:** From the junction, take the right fork immediately after the road to Camp Sloggett. Walk 0.6 miles to the end of the road, crossing over Elekeninui Stream and Maluapopoki Stream. Head south on the signed trail, descending into the vine-covered forest past ferns, blackberries and fragrant kahili ginger. The trail dips and rises as it parallels Kokee Stream below. The path then curves east, away from the stream to a plateau. The trail ends at the intersection with Kumuwela Road. Bear right on the road for 0.4 miles to Kumuwela Viewpoint on Kumuwela Ridge. The overlook provides views into Waimea Canyon and south to the ocean. Return along the same trail.

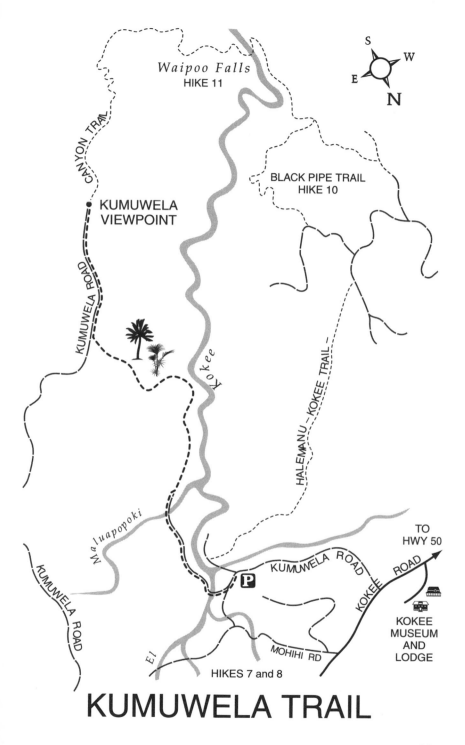

Waipoo Falls
HIKE 11

S W
E N

CANYON TRAIL

● KUMUWELA
VIEWPOINT

BLACK PIPE TRAIL
HIKE 10

KUMUWELA ROAD

Kokee

HALEMANU – KOKEE TRAIL –

Maluapopoki

KUMUWELA ROAD

TO HWY 50

P

KUMUWELA ROAD

KOKEE ROAD

KOKEE
MUSEUM
AND
LODGE

Ei

MOHIHI RD

HIKES 7 and 8

# KUMUWELA TRAIL

# Hike 9
# Halemanu—Kokee Trail

**Hiking distance:** 2.4 miles round trip
**Hiking time:** 1.5 hours
**Elevation gain:** 300 feet
**Maps:** U.S.G.S. Haena
       Trails of Kokee State Park

**Summary of hike:** Halemanu, which means "bird house" in Hawaiian, is a popular bird-watching route. The well-groomed trail meanders through a lush native forest dominated with koa, ohia and lehua trees. The trail connects the Halemanu Road with the Mohihi Road and may be combined with Hikes 10 or 11.

**Driving directions:** From the junction of Waimea Canyon Drive and Kokee Road in Waimea Canyon (directions to junction on page 14) drive 8.7 miles up the winding canyon to the Kokee Lodge and museum on the left. Continue 0.1 mile past the museum turnoff to Kumuwela Road, the first turnoff on the right after the lodge. (The road may be listed as Waineke Road on some maps.) Turn right and drive 0.5 miles to the signed "Camp Sloggett" turnoff on the right. Turn right and park by the old ranger station. The signed trail is on the right, just before the building.

**Hiking directions:** Hike southwest on the signed trail to the right of the old ranger station. The grassy trail winds through a beautiful forest with blackberry bushes, lantana and dense passion flower vines. The fairly level path follows the forested ridge with occasional views. Near the end of the trail is a quick descent to a junction with Halemanu Road. Return along the same path.

To hike further, bear left on the Halemanu Road and head south 0.4 miles to the junction on the left with the Cliff, Canyon and Black Pipe Trails (Hikes 10 and 11).

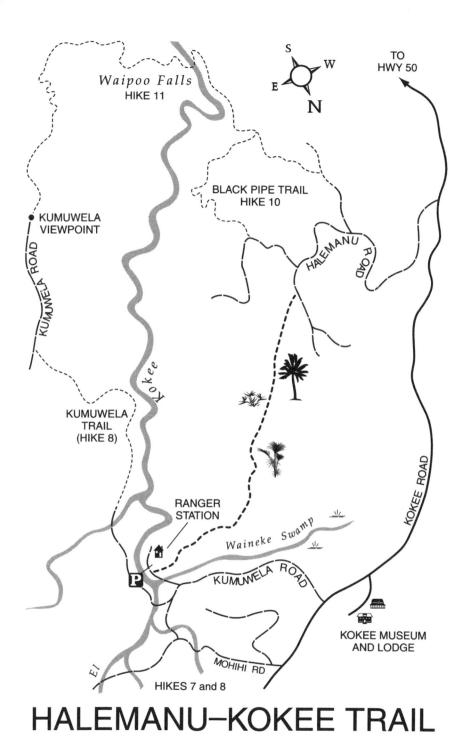

*Waipoo Falls*
HIKE 11

BLACK PIPE TRAIL
HIKE 10

S W
E N

TO
HWY 50

• KUMUWELA
VIEWPOINT

HALEMANU ROAD

KUMUWELA ROAD

*Kokee*

KUMUWELA
TRAIL
(HIKE 8)

KOKEE ROAD

RANGER
STATION

*Waineke Swamp*

P

KUMUWELA ROAD

KOKEE MUSEUM
AND LODGE

*Ei*

MOHIHI RD

HIKES 7 and 8

# HALEMANU–KOKEE TRAIL

# Hike 10
## Canyon—Black Pipe Loop

**Hiking distance:** 4 miles round trip
**Hiking time:** 2 hours
**Elevation gain:** 500 feet
**Maps:** U.S.G.S. Makaha Point, Haena and Waimea Canyon
     Trails of Kokee State Park

**Summary of hike:** This loop hike begins at the head of Waimea Canyon and follows a narrow shelf perched on the hillside overlooking the sheer cliffs and multi-colored walls of the canyon. The path traverses the east-facing cliffs through a lush tropical forest of koa, ohia and oak.

**Driving directions:** From the junction of Waimea Canyon Drive and Kokee Road in Waimea Canyon (directions to junction on page 14) drive 7.4 miles to Halemanu Road on the right. The road is located by the signed Cliff, Canyon and Black Pipe trailhead between mile markers 14 and 15. Parking is available on both sides of the road.

From Kokee Lodge and museum, drive 1.3 miles down canyon (south) to the signed trailhead.

**Hiking directions:** Hike downhill past the "Halemanu Valley Trails" sign on the unpaved road. On the valley floor, cross over Halemanu Stream and curve right, ascending the hill to a signed junction at 0.6 miles. Leave the Halemanu Road, and begin the loop hike on the right towards the Canyon Trail. The road soon becomes a footpath. Continue fifty yards to a signed junction with the Cliff Trail on the right. This spur trail is a wonderful detour for a great view of Waimea Canyon and the ocean. Back on the Canyon Trail, descend through the narrow draw on the right side of the Kokee irrigation ditch, built in 1923. Climb back up the hill to views of the multi-colored canyon walls and a signed junction. The right fork follows the Canyon Trail to Waipoo Falls (Hike 11). Take the left fork on the Black Pipe Trail, and traverse the hillside on the narrow path above Kokee

Stream. As the trail curves north (left), switchbacks lead uphill, reaching an old dirt road on the ridge. Follow the road to the left for a quarter mile, winding through the forest to a junction with the Halemanu Road. Again bear left, completing the loop at the Canyon Trail junction. Stay to the right, returning to the trailhead.

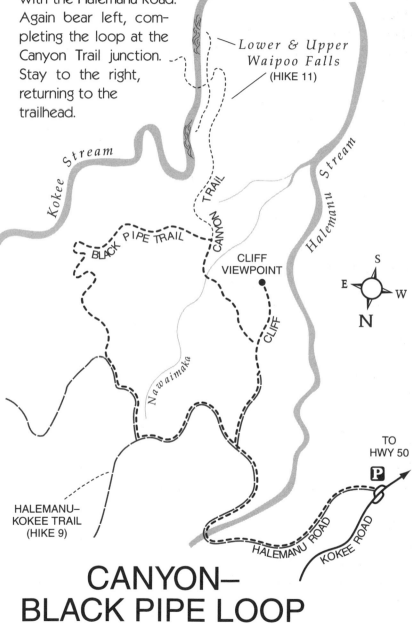

Lower & Upper Waipoo Falls (HIKE 11)

Kokee Stream

Halemanu Stream

BLACK PIPE TRAIL

CANYON TRAIL

CLIFF VIEWPOINT

CLIFF

Nawaimaka

S
E · W
N

TO HWY 50

P

HALEMANU–KOKEE TRAIL (HIKE 9)

HALEMANU ROAD

KOKEE ROAD

# CANYON–
# BLACK PIPE LOOP

# Hike 11
# Canyon Trail to Waipoo Falls

**Hiking distance:** 3.2 miles round trip
**Hiking time:** 1.5 hours
**Elevation gain:** 600 feet
**Maps:** U.S.G.S. Makaha Point, Haena and Waimea Canyon
Trails of Kokee State Park

**Summary of hike:** Upper and Lower Waipoo Falls offer a cool retreat for hikers in Waimea Canyon. Upper Waipoo Falls is fronted by a large swimming pool set in a tropical garden. Lower Waipoo Falls has showering cascades and several small soaking pools. The trail begins at the head of Waimea Canyon and follows the canyon's north rim past several panoramic overlooks. A short detour on the Cliff Trail offers additional views into the canyon.

**Driving directions:** From the junction of Waimea Canyon Drive and Kokee Road in Waimea Canyon (directions to junction on page 14) drive 7.4 miles to Halemanu Road on the right. The road is located by the signed Cliff, Canyon and Black Pipe trailhead between mile markers 14 and 15. Parking is available on both sides of the road.

From Kokee Lodge and museum, drive 1.3 miles down canyon (south) to the trailhead.

**Hiking directions:** Hike down the unpaved Halemanu Road to the valley floor. Cross over Halemanu Stream and curve to the right. Ascend the hill to a signed junction at 0.6 miles. Leave the Halemanu Road, and take the right fork towards the Canyon Trail. The road soon becomes a footpath. Fifty yards ahead is a signed junction with the Cliff Trail. This short spur trail leads to an overlook of Waimea Canyon. Back on the Canyon Trail, descend down a steep narrow gorge along the Kokee irrigation ditch. Climb up a short hill to a vista of the multi-colored canyon walls and a signed junction. The left fork is the Black Pipe Trail (Hike 10). Take the right fork, staying on the Canyon Trail to

an exposed, bare knoll overlooking the canyon. Pick up the trail
at the lower edge of the knoll on the left. Head downhill along
the eroded ridge, reaching a T-junction at Kokee Stream.
Take the left fork upstream to Upper Waipoo Falls
(Fall 1) and the pool. The main trail heads downstream to the two-tiered Lower Waipoo Falls
(Fall 2). Return along the same trail.

   To hike further, the Canyon Trail continues
to Kumuwela
Viewpoint,
Hike 8.

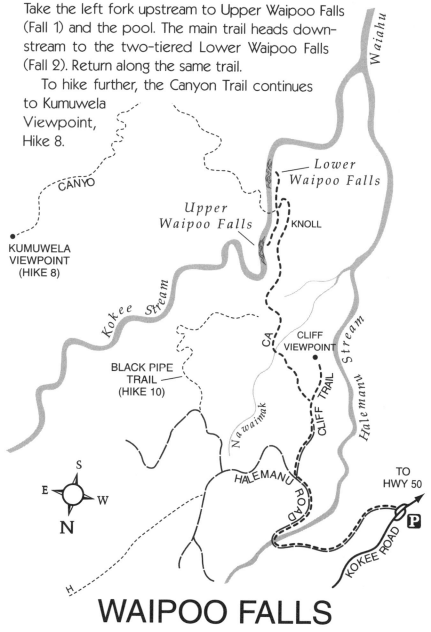

# WAIPOO FALLS

# Hike 12
# Milolii Ridge Trail

**Hiking distance:** 5 miles round trip
**Hiking time:** 2.5 hours
**Elevation gain:** 500 feet
**Maps:** U.S.G.S. Makaha Point
      Earthwalk Press Northwestern Kauai Recreation Map

**Summary of hike:** Milolii Ridge Trail follows a red dirt four-wheel drive road along a ridge through a lush forest of koa and ohia trees. The road extends five miles to the jagged cliffs overlooking Milolii Valley at the southern end of the Na Pali Coast. This hike follows the ridge for 2.5 miles to a picnic shelter under a canopy of trees in the Na Pali-Kona Forest Reserve. There are views across Makaha Ridge and the island of Niihau.

**Driving directions:** From the junction of Waimea Canyon Drive and Kokee Road in Waimea Canyon (directions to junction on page 14) drive 7.2 miles to Makaha Ridge Road on the left, between mile markers 13 and 14. Turn left and wind downhill 0.3 miles to the signed Milolii Ridge Road on the right. Park on the right by the trailhead

From Kokee Lodge and museum, drive 1.5 miles down canyon (south) to Makaha Ridge Road on the right.

**Hiking directions:** Head north past the metal gate on the unpaved road. There are mileage markers every quarter mile. The wide, red dirt path remains fairly level through a forest of koa and ohia for the first mile and then curves west. Along the way are a few dips and rises. At 1.4 miles the road becomes eroded and descends sharply, entering the Na Pali-Kona Forest Reserve at 1.75 miles. Views open to the west across Makaha Ridge and the island of Niihau. Just past 2.5 miles is the shady picnic shelter on the right. This is our turnaround spot.

To hike further, the trail steeply descends several times, reaching the edge of the cliffs in a pine forest overlooking Milolii Valley and the ocean.

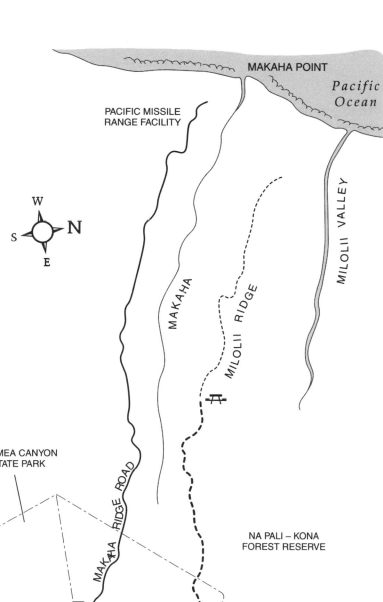

MAKAHA POINT

*Pacific Ocean*

PACIFIC MISSILE
RANGE FACILITY

MILOLII VALLEY

MAKAHA

MILOLII RIDGE

W
N
S
E

WAIMEA CANYON
STATE PARK

MAKAHA RIDGE ROAD

NA PALI – KONA
FOREST RESERVE

P

KA

KOKEE
STATE PARK

TO
HWY 50

KOKEE ROAD

HALEMANU ROAD
(HIKES 10 and      11)

TO
KOKEE LODGE/MUSEUM

# MILOLII RIDGE TRAIL

# Hike 13
# Iliau Nature Loop

**Hiking distance:** 0.3 mile loop
**Hiking time:** 15 minutes
**Elevation gain:** Level
**Maps:** U.S.G.S. Waimea Canyon
          Northwestern Kauai Recreational Map

**Summary of hike:** The Iliau Nature Loop is a short, self-guided path around a flat clearing on the dry western slope of Waimea Canyon. Several native plant species are identified with name plates. A covered picnic area and several benches are perched on the canyon's edge for great vistas into Waimea Canyon. Waialae Falls can be seen plunging off the cliffs across the gorge.

**Driving directions:** From the junction of Waimea Canyon Drive and Kokee Road in Waimea Canyon (directions to junction on page 14) drive north 1.8 miles to the signed trailhead on the right between mile markers 8 and 9. Parking pullouts are on the west (left) side of the road, directly across from the trailhead.

From Kokee Lodge and museum, drive 6.9 miles down canyon (south) to the parking area on the right.

**Hiking directions:** The Iliau Nature Loop and the Kukui Trail (Hikes 14 and 15) begin on the same path. Follow the trail to the right towards the edge of the canyon and a junction. The right fork descends into Waimea Canyon. Take the left fork on the Iliau Nature Loop, winding counterclockwise along the flat rim of the canyon. As the trail loops along the canyon rim, there are various vistas into and across the canyon. At a trail split, the right fork leads to an overlook and bench. The left fork curves back, returning to the trailhead.

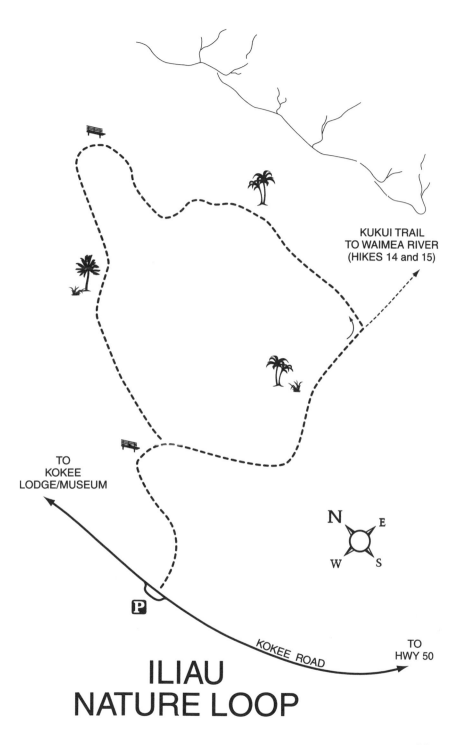

KUKUI TRAIL
TO WAIMEA RIVER
(HIKES 14 and 15)

TO
KOKEE
LODGE/MUSEUM

N
E
W
S

P

KOKEE ROAD

TO
HWY 50

# ILIAU
# NATURE LOOP

# Hike 14
# Kukui Trail to overlooks

**Hiking distance:** 2 miles round trip
**Hiking time:** 1.5 hours
**Elevation gain:** 750 feet
**Maps:** U.S.G.S. Waimea Canyon
      Earthwalk Press Northwestern Kauai Recreation Map

**Summary of hike:** This hike follows the first mile of the Kukui Trail into Waimea Canyon, descending to two spectacular viewpoints, each with a bench. Across the canyon are several waterfalls that stay in view throughout the one-mile descent. Waialae Falls is the dominant waterfall plunging off the cliffs. Wild goats are frequently visible along the canyon ridges.

**Driving directions:** From the junction of Waimea Canyon Drive and Kokee Road in Waimea Canyon (directions to junction on page 14) drive north 1.8 miles to the signed trailhead on the right between mile markers 8 and 9. Parking pullouts are on the west (left) side of the road, directly across from the trailhead.

From Kokee Lodge and museum, drive 6.9 miles down canyon (south) to the trailhead on the left.

**Hiking directions:** Follow the Iliau Nature Loop (Hike 13) on the right. After 100 yards, the nature loop bears left. Take the signed right fork on the Kukui Trail past the covered picnic area. Switchbacks lead downhill a quarter mile into the canyon to the first viewing area, graced with a bench. Quarter-mile markers are placed along the trail. Every step takes you deeper into the canyon and offers a changing view and perspective. Continue down to a second viewing area on an eroded promontory with a bench, just beyond the one-mile marker. The second viewing area is the turnaround point for this hike.

To hike further, the trail continues to the canyon floor at the Waimea River and Wiliwili Camp (Hike 15).

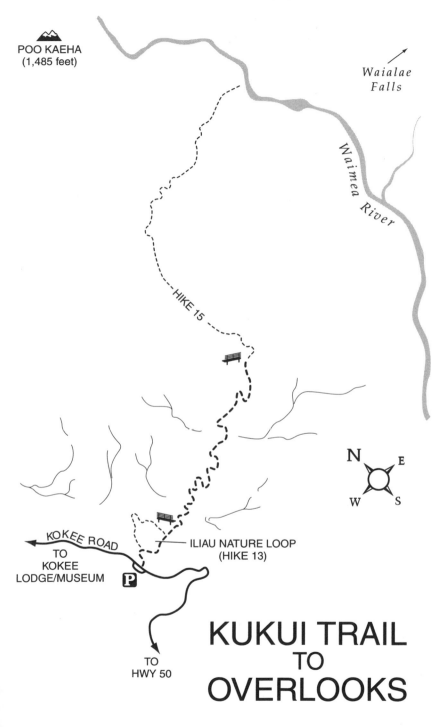

POO KAEHA
(1,485 feet)

Waialae
Falls

Waimea River

HIKE 15

N E
W S

KOKEE ROAD
TO
KOKEE
LODGE/MUSEUM

P

ILIAU NATURE LOOP
(HIKE 13)

TO
HWY 50

# KUKUI TRAIL
## TO
# OVERLOOKS

# Hike 15
## Kukui Trail to Waimea River

**Hiking distance:** 5 miles round trip
**Hiking time:** 3 hours
**Elevation gain:** 2,300 feet
**Maps:** U.S.G.S. Waimea Canyon
Earthwalk Press Northwestern Kauai Recreation Map

**Summary of hike:** The Kukui Trail is the shortest route to the base of Waimea Canyon. The steep descent drops 2,300 feet to the canyon floor at the Waimea River, following a series of switchbacks on the west canyon wall. The canyon views along the path continually change due to cloud cover, changing light, elevation and angles. The trail ends at Wiliwili Camp, a campsite with a covered shelter and table at the edge of the river.

**Driving directions:** From the junction of Waimea Canyon Drive and Kokee Road in Waimea Canyon (directions to junction on page 14) drive north 1.8 miles to the signed trailhead on the right between mile markers 8 and 9. Parking pullouts are on the west (left) side of the road, directly across from the trailhead.

From Kokee Lodge and museum, drive 6.9 miles down canyon (south) to the trailhead on the left.

**Hiking directions:** Follow the Iliau Nature Loop (Hike 13) on the right. After 100 yards, take the signed right fork on the Kukui Trail. Mileage markers are placed along the trail every quarter mile. Switchbacks lead steeply downhill along a ridge to a bench and viewing area at a quarter mile. Continue downhill to a second viewing area with a bench at one mile. Follow the ridgeline to a saddle. Bear left and head north down the bare hillside towards Poo Kaeha, the prominent formation to the north. Curve to the right, heading east into the forest. Zigzag downhill through the shady canopy, emerging at Wiliwili Camp and the Waimea River Trail. The river trail parallels the boulder-lined river in both directions. Downstream is a large pool. Return by climbing out of the canyon on the same trail.

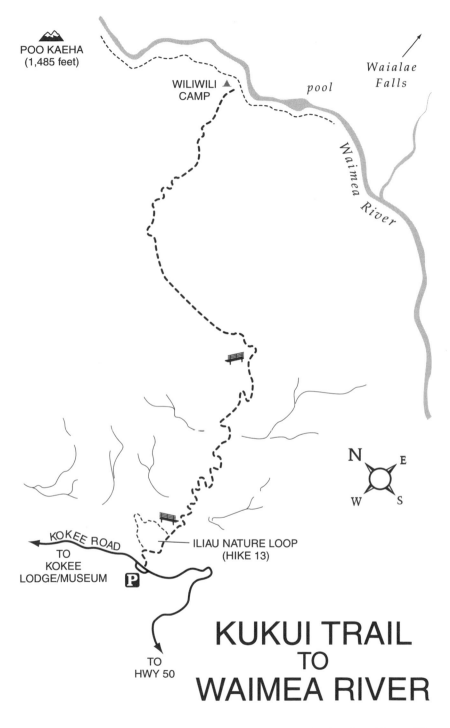

POO KAEHA
(1,485 feet)

WILIWILI
CAMP

Waialae
Falls

pool

Waimea River

N
E
W
S

KOKEE ROAD
TO
KOKEE
LODGE/MUSEUM

P

ILIAU NATURE LOOP
(HIKE 13)

TO
HWY 50

# KUKUI TRAIL
## TO
# WAIMEA RIVER

# Hike 16
# Russian Fort Elizabeth
# State Park

**Hiking distance:** 1 mile loop
**Hiking time:** 30 minutes
**Elevation gain:** Level
**Maps:** U.S.G.S. Kekaha and Hanapepe

**Summary of hike:** Russian Fort Elizabeth State Park is a 17-acre park just outside the town of Waimea. The fort is located at the mouth of the Waimea River, overlooking the ocean and the island of Niihau. The red rock walls of the fort were constructed in 1816 and were originally twelve feet high. Built without mortar, the walls are crumbling and fragile. The shell of the enclosure is all that remains.

**Driving directions:** From Lihue, drive 22.5 miles west on Highway 50. A sign is posted on the highway at the fort's entrance between mile markers 22 and 23. Turn left into the parking lot.

**Hiking directions:** From the parking lot, walk towards the map and history exhibit at the trailhead. Follow the trail to the right around the fort walls. This path leads to the east banks of the Waimea River. Continue the counterclockwise loop into the interior of the fort and past remnants of the guardrooms, barracks, cannon emplacements, the armory, and to the red rock stairs that lead to the lookout points along the coast. The trail loops around the fort, returning to the parking lot.

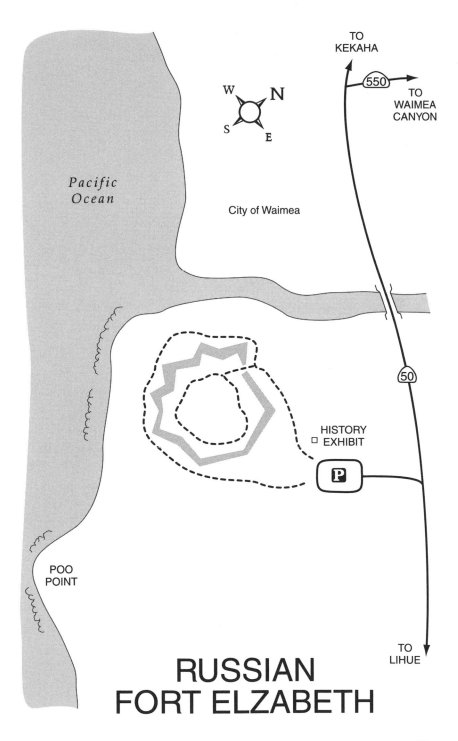

TO
KEKAHA

550

TO
WAIMEA
CANYON

W N
S E

*Pacific
Ocean*

City of Waimea

50

HISTORY
EXHIBIT

P

POO
POINT

TO
LIHUE

# RUSSIAN
# FORT ELZABETH

# Hike 17
# Kukuiolono Park and Gardens

**Hiking distance:** 1 mile round trip
**Hiking time:** 1 hour
**Elevation gain:** Level
**Maps:** U.S.G.S. Koloa

**Summary of hike:** Kukuiolono Park sits on a hill above the town of Kalaheo. The park, adjacent to a golf course, includes a 0.8-mile nature loop, a lava rock garden, a Hawaiian garden and a beautiful Japanese garden with a stone footbridge, sculptures, bonsai trees and fountains overgrown with plants. The trail is surrounded with ironwood and eucalyptus trees plus an abundance of flowers. The gardens are alive with domestic chickens that roam the grounds freely. The views extend to the neighboring hillsides dotted with homes and magnificent coastal views.

**Driving directions:** From Lihue, drive 12 miles west on Highway 50 to Papalina Road in the town of Kalaheo. Turn left (south) and continue one mile to Kukuiolono Park on the right. Turn right and park on the right for the nature loop trail. For the Japanese Garden, drive up the park road 0.2 miles to the parking lot at the end of the lane.

**Hiking directions:** To hike the nature loop, take the trail on the right parallel to Papalina Road. The well-defined path curves to the west in a pastoral setting through a shady, mature forest. The trail loops counterclockwise, returning to the parking area.

For the Japanese, Hawaiian and rock gardens, walk slightly uphill to the various walkways which loop through the gardens. All three gardens are bordered by the golf course.

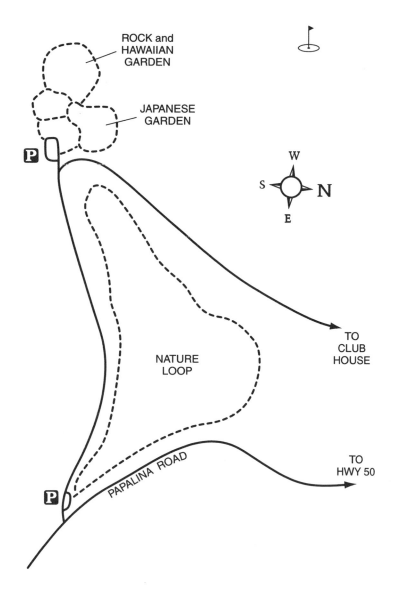

ROCK and
HAWAIIAN
GARDEN

JAPANESE
GARDEN

P

W
S ◆ N
E

NATURE
LOOP

TO
CLUB
HOUSE

PAPALINA ROAD

P

TO
HWY 50

# KUKUIOLONO PARK
## AND
# GARDENS

# Hike 18
# Poipu Beach Park and tidepools

**Hiking distance:** 2 miles round trip
**Hiking time:** 1 hours
**Elevation gain:** Level
**Maps:** U.S.G.S. Koloa

**Summary of hike:** This is more than a hike—it is an excellent place to spend the day exploring, enjoying water sports and sunbathing. Poipu is located on the southernmost point in Kauai. The popular crescent-shaped beach park is protected by off-shore reefs between two rocky points. The park sits in a small bay with grassy knolls and sandy beaches. To the east, lava formations house tidepools containing a variety of small fish, crabs and hermit crabs. Ocean waves crash against the cliffs and blowholes spout like geysers.

**Driving directions:** From Lihue, drive 6.5 miles west on Highway 50 to Manuhia Road/Highway 520 between mile markers 6 and 7. Turn left and drive through the eucalyptus "Tree Tunnel." Head 3.3 miles to Koloa Road in the town of Koloa. Turn right and make a quick left onto Poipu Beach Road. Continue 2.5 miles to Hoowili Road and turn right. Go 0.2 miles to the oceanfront. Several parking lots are available.

**Hiking directions:** From the parking area, walk towards the ocean and Poipu Beach Park. To the right is Nu Kumoi Point, a narrow strip of sand jutting out into the water. Excellent snorkeling can be found on the west side of the point. To the left (east) of Poipu Beach Park, there are abundant tidepools and blowholes on the lava formations. Petroglyphs can be seen along the cliff walls at low tide, although property development has made access difficult. Walk along the lava formations and explore at your own pace.

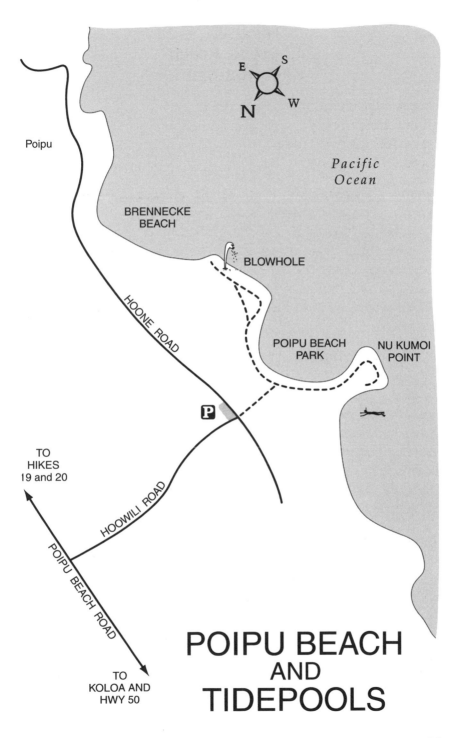

Poipu

E ─ S
N ─ W

*Pacific
Ocean*

BRENNECKE
BEACH

BLOWHOLE

HOONE ROAD

POIPU BEACH
PARK

NU KUMOI
POINT

**P**

TO
HIKES
19 and 20

HOOWILI ROAD

POIPU BEACH ROAD

TO
KOLOA AND
HWY 50

# POIPU BEACH
## AND
# TIDEPOOLS

# Hike 19
# Shipwreck Beach
# Keoniloa Bay

**Hiking distance:** 2 miles round trip
**Hiking time:** 1 hour
**Elevation gain:** 50 feet
**Maps:** U.S.G.S. Koloa

**Summary of hike:** Shipwreck Beach, in Keoniloa Bay, is a half-mile crescent of sandy beach. The bay sits between the lava rocks of Kaneaukai and the lithified sand dune bluff of Makawehi Point. Trails crisscross the Makawehi cliffs, offering commanding views out to sea. Exploring the cliffs leads to beautifully sculpted rock formations, coves, caves, tidepools and magnificent views up the rugged coastline and the Hoary Head Range.

**Driving directions:** From Lihue, drive 6.5 miles west on Highway 50 to Manuhia Road/Highway 520 between mile markers 6 and 7. Turn left and drive through the eucalyptus "Tree Tunnel." Head 3.3 miles to Koloa Road in the town of Koloa. Turn right and make a quick left onto Poipu Beach Road. Continue 3.6 miles to Ainako Street, just past the Hyatt Regency Kauai, and turn right. (Poipu Beach Road becomes Weliweli Road en route.) Go 0.2 miles to the public parking lot on the right at the beachfront.

**Hiking directions:** Walk down to the sand beach, and bear left towards the large Makawehi bluffs, jutting out into the ocean. Along the back side of the sandy beach, a forested path leads to the lithified sandstone cliffs. Several paths lead up to the promontory overlooking the ocean. A myriad of paths comb the formation through groves of twisted ironwood trees, vegetated sand dunes and across the barren rock cliffs. Trails follow the cliff's edge and climb up to the sandy summit. Follow your own route, choosing your turnaround spot.

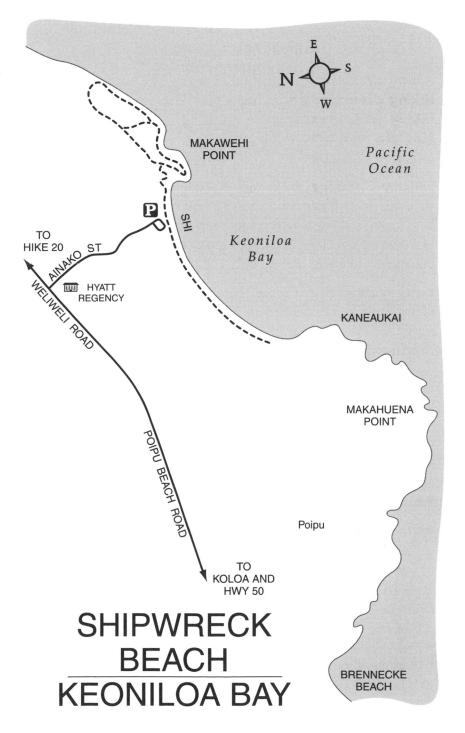

N E S W

MAKAWEHI POINT

*Pacific Ocean*

P

SHI

TO HIKE 20

AINAKO ST

*Keoniloa Bay*

WELIWELI ROAD

HYATT REGENCY

KANEAUKAI

POIPU BEACH ROAD

MAKAHUENA POINT

Poipu

TO KOLOA AND HWY 50

# SHIPWRECK BEACH
# KEONILOA BAY

BRENNECKE BEACH

# Hike 20
# Mahaulepu Beach to Kawelikoa Point

**Hiking distance:** 5 miles round trip
**Hiking time:** 2.5 hours
**Elevation gain:** 100 feet
**Maps:** U.S.G.S. Koloa and Lihue

**Summary of hike:** The trail from Mahaulepu Beach follows isolated 100-foot cliffs to Kawelikoa Point, passing weather-sculpted rock formations, sharp pinnacles, coves and caves, blowholes, natural bridges and awesome coastal views. The views extend across the high mountain ridges of the Haupu (Hoary Head) Range and up the scalloped coastline.

**Driving directions:** From Lihue, drive 6.5 miles west on Highway 50 to Manuhia Road/Highway 520 between mile markers 6 and 7. Turn left and drive through the eucalyptus "Tree Tunnel." Head 3.3 miles to Koloa Road in the town of Koloa. Turn right and make a quick left onto Poipu Beach Road. Continue 5.3 miles (the pavement ends after 3.7 miles and becomes Weliweli Road) to a 4-way junction. Turn right and drive 0.4 miles to a T-junction. The beach access parking area is on the right.

**Hiking directions:** The well-defined path leads through a lush forest to the sandy, tree-lined beach. To the right, the steep cliffs of Punahoa Point extend out into the sea. At the base of the cliffs are tidepools. Paths lead up the cliffs to scenic overlooks. To the other side of Mahaulepu Beach, follow the shoreline between the ocean and the trees. Walk 0.3 miles northeast, crossing the dunes at Kamala Point into Kawailoa Bay. At the east end of the bay are sculpted lava formations. Paths cross the tree-covered cliffs to Haula Beach, a pocket beach between Paoo and Naakea Points. The wild beauty of the eroded cliffs and crashing surf is truly spectacular. The trail crosses the cliffs, reaching Kawelikoa Point at 2.5 miles. Return along the same path.

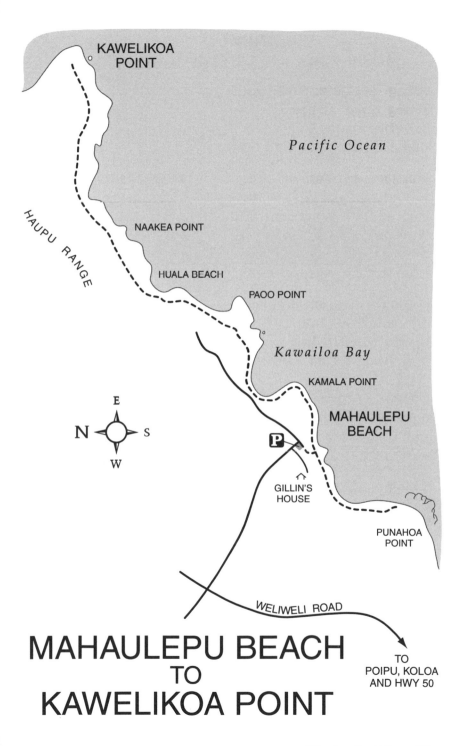

KAWELIKOA POINT

Pacific Ocean

HAUPU RANGE

NAAKEA POINT

HUALA BEACH

PAOO POINT

Kawailoa Bay

KAMALA POINT

MAHAULEPU BEACH

P

GILLIN'S HOUSE

PUNAHOA POINT

WELIWELI ROAD

TO POIPU, KOLOA AND HWY 50

E
N S
W

# MAHAULEPU BEACH
## TO
# KAWELIKOA POINT

# Hike 21
# Kipu Falls

**Hiking distance:** 1 mile round trip
**Hiking time:** 30 minutes
**Elevation gain:** 50 feet
**Maps:** U.S.G.S. Koloa

**Summary of hike:** Kipu Falls is a 20-foot waterfall plunging into a large, deep pool ringed by 20-foot cliffs. The trail follows a cane road parallel to Huleia Stream, a large body of water cascading through the forest. The jagged mountain ridges of the Haupu Range serve as a backdrop to the cane fields. On the weekends, locals dive and swim here, but be extremely cautious, as the footing on the cliffs around the pool can be treacherous.

**Driving directions:** From Lihue, drive 3 miles west on Highway 50 to Kipu Road across from mile marker 3. Turn left (south) and drive 0.4 miles to a road fork. Bear right on the unpaved Kipu Road 0.7 miles to a parking pullout on the right by the "one lane bridge" sign.

**Hiking directions:** The trail is the gated cane road that is directly across the road. The gate has an ancient, scratched out and disregarded "No Trespass" sign. Walk around the opening on the right side of the gate. Head south on the dirt road, following the watercourse of Huleia Stream on the right. Several side paths lead down to the stream. As you near the roaring waterfall, the cane is tall, blocking the view. Watch for a narrow opening in the brush. Bear right and descend to the top of the waterfall on the cliffs above the pool. This is the best access point from the steep cliffs. If you continue on the main trail a short distance, a second access leads to an overlook of Kipu Falls and the large pool. Return by retracing your steps.

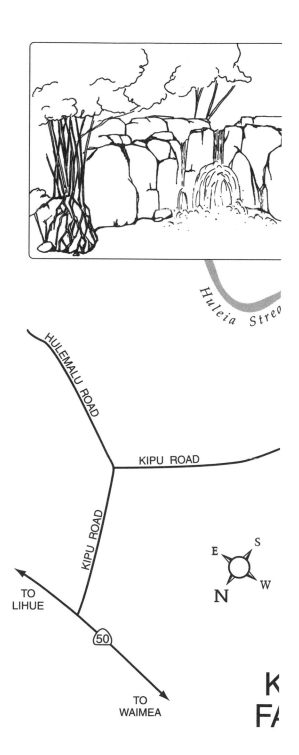

HULEMALU ROAD

KIPU ROAD

KIPU ROAD

Huleia Stream

TO
LIHUE

50

TO
WAIMEA

E  S
N  W

K
F/

# Hike 22
# Wailua Falls

**Hiking distance:** View from road (no hiking)
                        or hazardous 1.5 mile round trip hike
**Hiking time:** 1 hour
**Elevation gain:** 100 feet
**Maps:** U.S.G.S. Kapaa

**Summary of hike:** Wailua Falls is a powerful, dramatic 80-foot waterfall. The twin falls (cover photo) plunges into a pool surrounded by lush vegetation. It was filmed in the opening sequence of the *Fantasy Island* television series. The falls is viewed from the side of the road. A difficult and dangerous hike descends on an unmaintained, slippery trail. After the descent, the wet path follows the South Fork of the Wailua River upstream to the pool at the base of the falls.

**Driving directions:** From Lihue, drive north on Highway 56 one mile to Highway 583. Turn left. A large highway sign will direct you. Continue 4 miles to the end of the road.

**Hiking directions:** The Wailua Falls viewing area is on the right side of the road. For those with a throw-caution-to-the-wind desire for the ultimate nature photo, a steep, hazardous trail descends to the base of the falls. Hiking this unmaintained trail is not recommended. For those who do not follow sound advice, the trailhead is 0.2 miles back down the road from the waterfall guard railing. Park in the dirt parking area on the east side of the road. After the steep descent, using roots and branches for assistance, the path reaches the South Fork Wailua River. Bear left on the wet, slippery path, crossing a dangerous rock ledge at the river's edge. Head upriver through the forest canopy to the base of the waterfall and large pool. Return along the same path.

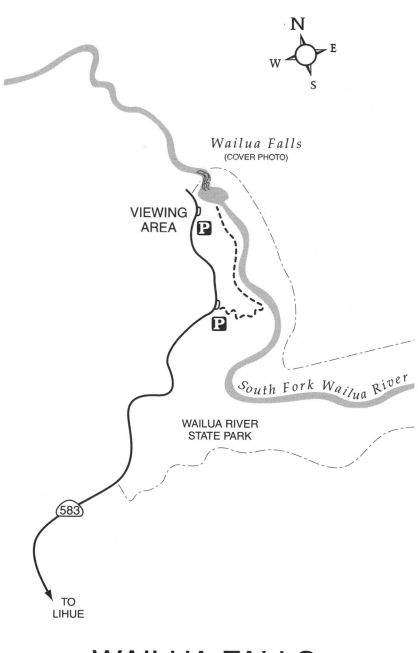

N
E
W
S

*Wailua Falls*
(COVER PHOTO)

VIEWING
AREA

**P**

**P**

*South Fork Wailua River*

WAILUA RIVER
STATE PARK

583

TO
LIHUE

# WAILUA FALLS

# Hike 23
## Lydgate State Park

**Hiking distance:** 2 miles round trip
**Hiking time:** 1 hour
**Elevation gain:** Level
**Maps:** U.S.G.S. Kapaa

**Summary of hike:** Lydgate Park is a popular 40-acre ocean-front park at the mouth of the Wailua River. The long stretch of sand fronts a beautiful grass park with picnic areas, facilities and groves of ironwood trees. Two sandy, boulder-enclosed ponds are ideal for kids and snorkeling. Near the river at the north end of the park are the ruins of Hauola (City of Refuge) and Hikina A Ka La (Rising of the Sun), two sacred religious sites from the 1300s. An interpretive trail circles the temple through a coconut grove. The views inland include the Nounou Mountains and the Kalepa Ridge.

**Driving directions:** From Lihue, drive 5.7 miles north on Highway 56 to Leho Drive on the right, just before crossing the Wailua River. The turnoff, located between mile marker 5 and 6, is marked with a large "Lydgate Beach Park" sign. Turn right and drive down to the north (far) end of the parking lot.

**Hiking directions:** Walk north to the mouth of the Wailua River. An interpretive trail circles the two adjacent *heiaus* (temples) along the river and around a knoll. Head south parallel to the shoreline past an oval pool built with black lava boulders. Continue past the pools, following the sandy beach or the tree-lined grassy park. At the south end of the park, a trail continues along the back side of the shoreline past some lava rocks to a series of tree-lined beaches. Choose your own turnaround point.

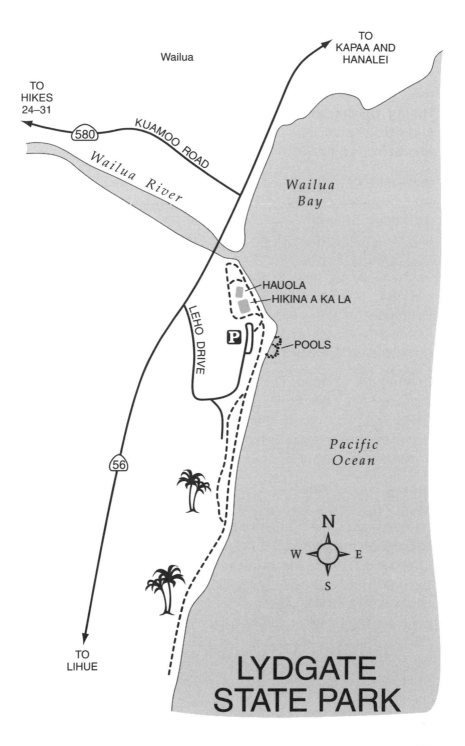

Wailua

TO
KAPAA AND
HANALEI

TO
HIKES
24–31

580  KUAMOO ROAD

*Wailua River*

*Wailua
Bay*

HAUOLA
HIKINA A KA LA

P

LEHO DRIVE

POOLS

56

*Pacific
Ocean*

N
W E
S

TO
LIHUE

LYDGATE
STATE PARK

# Hike 24
# Powerline Trail
# (southern access)

**Hiking distance:** 5 miles round trip
**Hiking time:** 2.5 hours
**Elevation gain:** 800 feet
**Maps:** U.S.G.S. Waialeale
      Recreation Map of Eastern Kauai

**Summary of hike:** The Powerline Trail is a 10.5-mile trail that links the interior valleys with the north shore at Princeville. The trail, which follows powerlines, is a dirt road cut through the wilderness. The trail runs along the east side of Mount Waialeale, the wettest spot on earth. This hike from the southern trailhead follows the first 2.5 miles of the muddy trail to an overlook with views of two beautiful waterfalls. For a strenuous all-day event, this trail can be combined with Hike 46 for a fantastic one-way shuttle hike.

**Driving directions:** From Lihue, drive six miles north on Highway 56 to Kuamoo Road/Highway 580, the first intersection after crossing the Wailua River. Turn left and continue 6.9 miles to the Keahua Arboretum. There are parking lots on both sides of the road. You may park here and walk a quarter mile to the trailhead, or drive across the Keahua Stream and park on the right by the signed trailhead.

**Hiking directions:** Walk northwest past the arboretum on Highway 580. Wade across Keahua Stream to the signed trail on the right (north) side of the road at a quarter mile. Take the trail to the right and head up the rocky road. At the top of the first hill, a second access route joins the main trail. Stay to the right, dodging muddy pools on the vividly red clay road. To the west are views (weather permitting) of Kawaikini, the summit of Kauai at 5,243 feet, and Mount Waialeale. The jagged peaks of the Haupu (Hoary Head) Ridge can be seen to the southeast beyond Lihue. Continue northbound on the undulating path

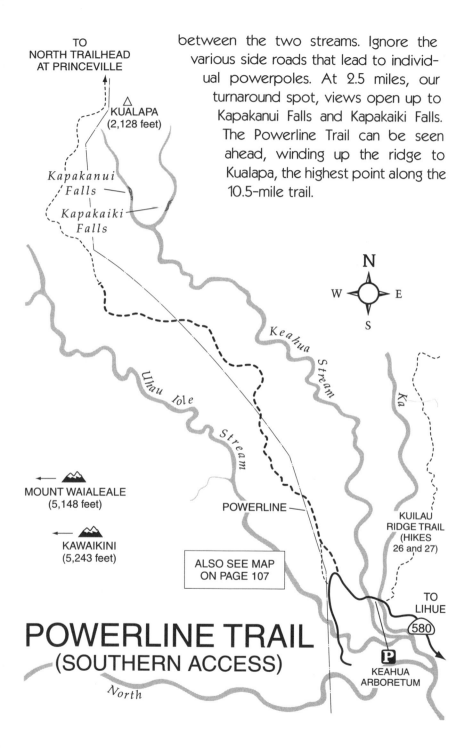

between the two streams. Ignore the various side roads that lead to individual powerpoles. At 2.5 miles, our turnaround spot, views open up to Kapakanui Falls and Kapakaiki Falls. The Powerline Trail can be seen ahead, winding up the ridge to Kualapa, the highest point along the 10.5-mile trail.

TO
NORTH TRAILHEAD
AT PRINCEVILLE

△
KUALAPA
(2,128 feet)

*Kapakanui
Falls*

*Kapakaiki
Falls*

N
W — E
S

*Keahua Stream*

*Uhau Iole*

*Stream*

*Ka*

MOUNT WAIALEALE
(5,148 feet)

KAWAIKINI
(5,243 feet)

POWERLINE

KUILAU
RIDGE TRAIL
(HIKES
26 and 27)

ALSO SEE MAP
ON PAGE 107

TO
LIHUE
580

POWERLINE TRAIL
(SOUTHERN ACCESS)

*North*

P
KEAHUA
ARBORETUM

# Hike 25
## Keahua Arboretum
## and Opaekaa Falls

**Hiking distance:** 0.5 miles round trip
**Hiking time:** 30 minutes
**Elevation gain:** Level
**Maps:** U.S.G.S. Waialeale
         Recreational Map of Eastern Kauai

**Summary of hike:** The 30-acre Keahua Arboretum is located in the mountains above Wailua. This quiet refuge includes expansive open lawns with sheltered picnic areas surrounded by mountains and lush forests. The arboretum is divided into two areas by Keahua Stream, which runs through the middle of the arboretum. The bubbling stream features two large swimming holes. Trails follow along the water on both sides of the stream.

**Driving directions:** From Lihue, drive six miles north on Highway 56 to Kuamoo Road/Highway 580, the first intersection after crossing the Wailua River. Turn left and continue 6.9 miles to the Keahua Arboretum. There are parking lots on both sides of the road.

Stop at Opaekaa Falls en route, just under two miles along Kuamoo Road. (See map on page 75.) A short walk leads to an overlook of a beautiful waterfall plunging hundreds of feet into a pool. Across the road is Wailua River State Park, with an overlook of the forest-lined Wailua River backed by the Kalepa Forest Reserve. Poliahu, an ancient Hawaiian *heiau*, is upstream.

**Hiking directions:** This nature walk through the arboretum begins on the south end of the parking area. Wander through the lush park grounds past groves of gum trees, hau thickets and a wide variety of exotic tropical plants, both native and introduced. The paths follow both banks of Keahua Stream to swimming holes and picnic tables a short distance downstream. To reach the trails on the west, wade across Keahua Stream on the road by the parking area.

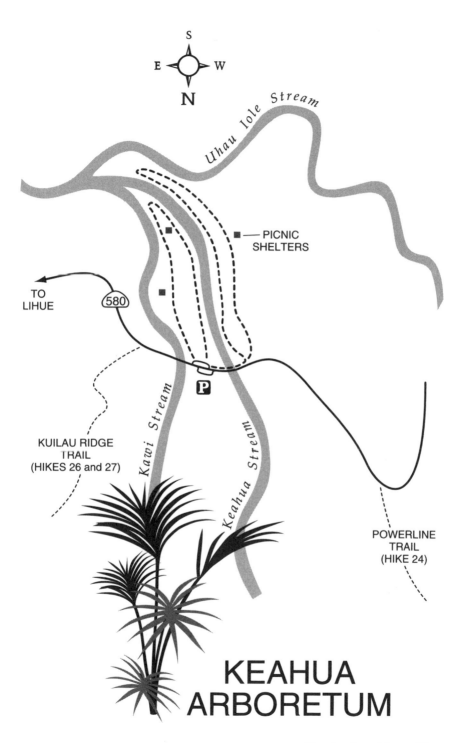

S
E · W
N

*Uhau Iole Stream*

PICNIC SHELTERS

TO LIHUE

580

P

KUILAU RIDGE TRAIL
(HIKES 26 and 27)

*Kawi Stream*

*Keahua Stream*

POWERLINE TRAIL
(HIKE 24)

# KEAHUA ARBORETUM

# Hike 26
# Kuilau Ridge Trail to overlook

**Hiking distance:** 2.4 miles round trip
**Hiking time:** 1.5 hours
**Elevation gain:** 400 feet
**Maps:** U.S.G.S. Waialeale and Kapaa
Recreational Map of Eastern Kauai

**Summary of hike:** This hike follows the first section of the forested Kuilau Ridge Trail (Hike 27), an old 4-wheel drive road. This path leads to a picnic shelter and overlook on a grassy plateau with impressive views. The panoramas extend west across the lush hillsides and beautiful valley to Mount Waialeale (weather permitting) and seaward to Nounou Mountain and Hoary Head.

**Driving directions:** From Lihue, drive six miles north on Highway 56 to Kuamoo Road/Highway 580, the first intersection after crossing the Wailua River. Turn left and continue 6.9 miles to the Keahua Arboretum. There are parking lots on both sides of the road.

**Hiking directions:** From the Keahua Arboretum, walk back along the road 100 yards to the signed trail on the left (north) side of the road. Bear left, leaving the valley, and ascend the ridge on the old road above Kawi Stream. Heading north, the trail skirts the ridge on the east. Stay on the main trail, passing various side paths. A large, flat grassy area with a sheltered picnic table is reached at 1.2 miles. From this resting spot, there are beautiful panoramic views of the many ridges and valleys. There are more stunning vistas within the next quarter mile. After relaxing and savoring the views, return along the same trail.

To hike further, the Kuilau Ridge Trail continues to a junction on a small knoll with the Moalepe Trail (Hike 27).

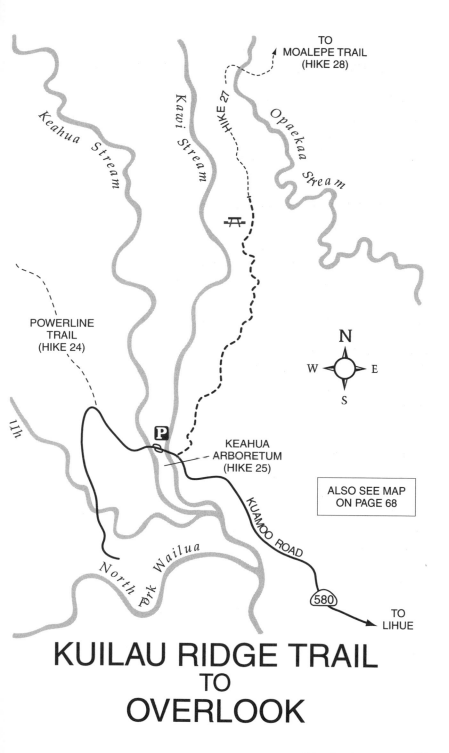

TO
MOALEPE TRAIL
(HIKE 28)

*Keahua Stream*

*Kawi Stream*

HIKE 27

*Opaekaa Stream*

POWERLINE
TRAIL
(HIKE 24)

11h

N

W &#x2756; E

S

**P**

KEAHUA
ARBORETUM
(HIKE 25)

ALSO SEE MAP
ON PAGE 68

KUAMOO ROAD

*North Fork Wailua*

580

TO
LIHUE

# KUILAU RIDGE TRAIL
## TO
# OVERLOOK

# Hike 27
# Kuilau Ridge Trail to Moalepe Trail

**Hiking distance:** 4.4 miles round trip
**Hiking time:** 2.5 hours
**Elevation gain:** 700 feet
**Maps:** U.S.G.S. Waialeale and Kapaa
　　　Recreational Map of Eastern Kauai

map
next page

**Summary of hike:** The Kuilau Ridge Trail begins at the Keahua Arboretum (Hike 25) and climbs a forested ridge in the Lihue-Koloa Forest Reserve. Along the way, panoramic views open up across the rolling hillsides and picturesque valley to Mount Waialeale to the west, the Makaleha Mountains to the north and the Pacific Ocean to the east. This trail can be combined with the Moalepe Trail (Hike 28) for a one-way, 4.6-mile shuttle hike.

**Driving directions:** From Lihue, drive six miles north on Highway 56 to Kuamoo Road/Highway 580, the first intersection after crossing the Wailua River. Turn left and continue 6.9 miles to the Keahua Arboretum. There are parking lots on both sides of the road.

**Hiking directions:** Follow the hiking directions for Hike 26 to the picnic shelter and overlook. From the picnic shelter, continue up the ridge. The winding path zigzags along a narrow ridge between Kawi Stream and Opaekaa Stream. To the east is a wonderful view of Nounou (Sleeping Giant) Mountain and the ocean at Kapaa. Cross a wooden footbridge over Opaekaa Stream, and climb up to the ridge in a clearing. Follow the Kamoohoopulu Ridge for 2.1 miles to the Moalepe Trail. The trail junction is on a small, flat grassy knoll by an old metal "End Kuilau Trail" sign. From the knoll are close-up views of the Makaleha Mountains. To the right is the Moalepe Trail (Hike 28).

# Hike 28
# Moalepe Trail to Kuilau Ridge Trail

**Hiking distance:** 5 miles round trip
**Hiking time:** 2.5 hours
**Elevation gain:** 700 feet
**Maps:** U.S.G.S. Kapaa
      Recreational Map of Eastern Kauai

map
next page

**Summary of hike:** The Moalepe Trail climbs up to the Kuilau Ridge in the foothills of the Makaleha Mountains. The first mile crosses pastureland on a red dirt road with panoramas of the lush, green jagged canyons and ridges of the Makaleha Mountains. Moalepe Stream winds its way down the valley on the north side of the trail. The trail ends at a junction with the Kuilau Ridge Trail (Hike 27) in the forest reserve. These two trails can be combined for a one-way, 4.6-mile shuttle hike.

**Driving directions:** From Lihue, drive six miles north on Highway 56 to Kuamoo Road/Highway 580, the first intersection after crossing the Wailua River. Turn left and continue 2.8 miles to Kamalu Road/Highway 581. Turn right and drive 1.6 miles to Olohena Road. Turn left and go 1.6 miles to the end of the paved road at the intersection with Waipouli Road. Park in the pullout on the left by the signed Moalepe Trail.

**Hiking directions:** Hike northwest on the red dirt road, gently gaining elevation. The road is a right-of-way through private property to the forest reserve boundary. Cross the open country and pastureland to the end of the fenceline at 1.1 mile. Follow the muddy trail as it twists and curves up the narrowing mountain ridge towards Kuilau Ridge. At 2.5 miles, the trail ends on Kamoohoopulu Ridge at a small, flat grassy knoll above Moalepe Stream. From the knoll are close-up views of the Makaleha Mountains. A short distance to the left is an old metal "End Kuilau Trail" sign, our turnaround spot. This is where the Moalepe Trail connects with the Kuilau Ridge Trail from the south (Hike 27).

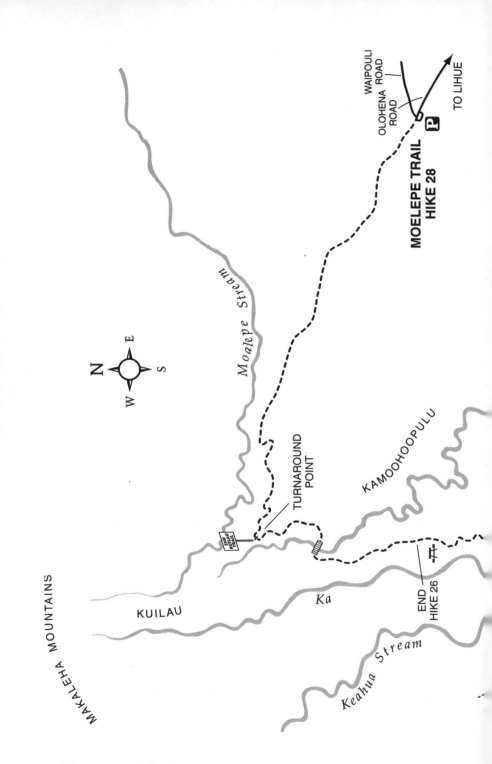

WAIPOULI ROAD

OLOHENA ROAD

TO LIHUE

**P**

**MOELEPE TRAIL**
**HIKE 28**

*Moalepe Stream*

N
E
S
W

TURNAROUND
POINT

END
KUILAU
TRAIL

KAMOOHOOPULU

*Ka*

KUILAU

END
HIKE 26

MAKALEHA MOUNTAINS

*Keahua Stream*

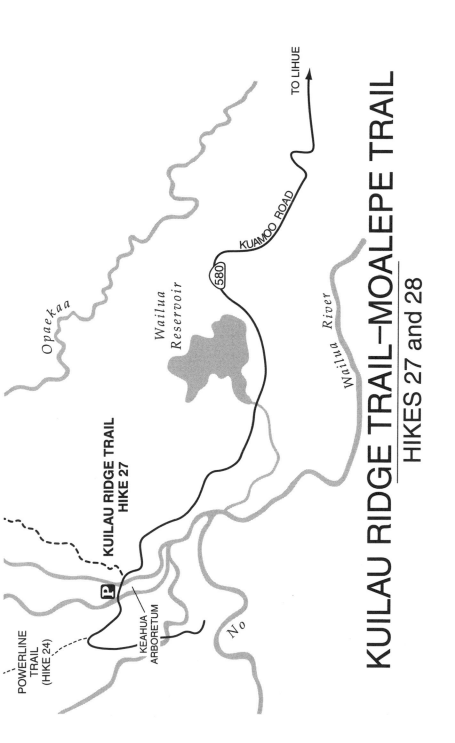

KUILAU RIDGE TRAIL–MOALEPE TRAIL
HIKES 27 and 28

# Hike 29
# Nounou Mountain Trail West to Alii Vista Hale
## "Sleeping Giant"

**Hiking distance:** 3 miles round trip
**Hiking time:** 1.5 hours
**Elevation gain:** 800 feet
**Maps:** U.S.G.S. Kapaa
       Recreational Map of Eastern Kauai

**Summary of hike:** The Nounou Mountain Trail West is one of the three trails that climb to the summit of Nounou Mountain, known as Sleeping Giant. The hike begins on the west side of the mountain and climbs through the forest to Alii Vista Hale, a picnic shelter and overlook at the summit. The summit has great views of the Makaleha Mountains, Mount Waialeale, the Wailua River, the Coconut Coast and the seacoast communities.

**Driving directions:** From Lihue, drive six miles north on Highway 56 to Kuamoo Road/Highway 580, the first intersection after crossing the Wailua River. Turn left and continue 2.8 miles to Kamalu Road/Highway 581. Turn right and drive 1.2 miles to the signed Nounou Mountain Trail West on the right (next to 1055 Kamalu Road) and park.

**Hiking directions:** Head east on the wide forest reserve right-of-way between rows of private homes and a cattle ranch. This public access trail reaches the forested footpath at the base of Nounou Mountain at 0.3 miles. Head uphill, weaving through a canopy of guava and oak trees to a signed junction in a distinct grove of Norfolk Island pines. The Kuamoo-Nounou Trail (Hike 31) is straight ahead. Curve left through a lane bordered by two parallel rows of Norfolk Island pines. Switchbacks lead up the steep trail along the contours of the mountain. At 1.4 miles, the West Trail ends at a junction with the East Trail (Hike 32). Take the right fork on the Nounou Mountain Trail East to Alii Vista Hale, a picnic shelter on a grassy knoll. After enjoying the panoramas, return along the same trail.

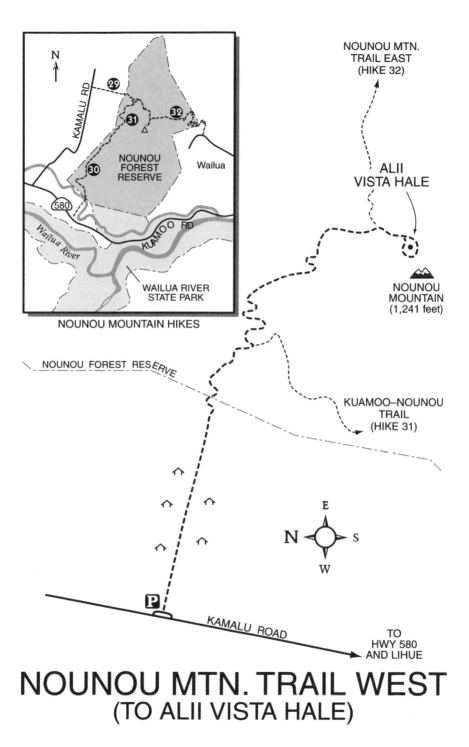

NOUNOU MTN.
TRAIL EAST
(HIKE 32)

N

KAMALU RD

㉙

㉛ ㉜

NOUNOU
FOREST
RESERVE

Wailua

㉚

580

KUAMOO RD

Wailua River

WAILUA RIVER
STATE PARK

NOUNOU MOUNTAIN HIKES

ALII
VISTA HALE

NOUNOU
MOUNTAIN
(1,241 feet)

NOUNOU FOREST RESERVE

KUAMOO–NOUNOU
TRAIL
(HIKE 31)

E
N ◈ S
W

P

KAMALU ROAD

TO
HWY 580
AND LIHUE

# NOUNOU MTN. TRAIL WEST
## (TO ALII VISTA HALE)

# Hike 30
# Kuamoo—Nounou Trail to Valley Vista Hale
# Nounou Mountain "Sleeping Giant"

**Hiking distance:** 1.5 miles round trip
**Hiking time:** 1 hour
**Elevation gain:** 150 feet
**Maps:** U.S.G.S. Kapaa
        Recreational Map of Eastern Kauai

**Summary of hike:** This beautiful mountain path, which leads to panoramic views, follows the first portion of the Kuamoo-Nounou Trail for a short walk into the Nounou reserve. The hike begins on the valley floor by Opaekaa Stream, a half mile upstream from the waterfall. The trail crosses a footbridge over the stream and leads to Valley Vista Hale, a grassy vista point with a sheltered picnic table perched on the side of the mountain. From the overlook are views of the Kalepa Ridge across the Wailua River, Lihue Basin and the Makaleha Mountains.

**Driving directions:** From Lihue, drive six miles north on Highway 56 to Kuamoo Road/Highway 580, the first intersection after crossing the Wailua River. Turn left and continue 2.4 miles to the parking area on the right. The parking area is 0.7 miles past Opaekaa Falls, directly across from Nelia Street.

**Hiking directions:** From the parking area, a sign on the fence marks the trailhead. Follow the tree-lined lane 0.2 miles to the footbridge over Opaekaa Stream. After crossing, the trail curves left along a fenceline, then winds its way up the side of Nounou Mountain into a dense forest canopy. A short distance ahead, the trail breaks out of the forest to views of the Lihue Basin. At 0.75 miles you will be treated to Valley Vista Hale, a picnic shelter and overlook. This is the turnaround point. After resting and savoring the views, return along the same trail.

To hike further, the Kuamoo-Nounou Trail continues another mile up the mountain to a junction with the Nounou Mountain Trail West (Hike 31).

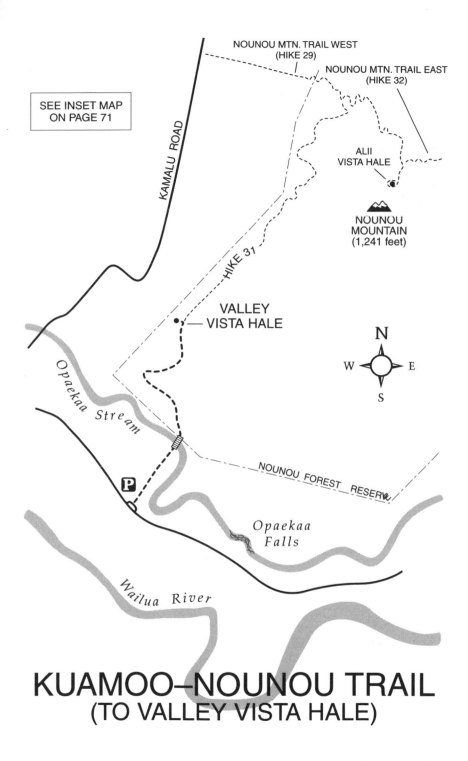

SEE INSET MAP
ON PAGE 71

NOUNOU MTN. TRAIL WEST
(HIKE 29)

NOUNOU MTN. TRAIL EAST
(HIKE 32)

KAMALU ROAD

HIKE 31

ALII
VISTA HALE

NOUNOU
MOUNTAIN
(1,241 feet)

VALLEY
VISTA HALE

N
W — E
S

*Opaekaa Stream*

**P**

NOUNOU FOREST RESERVE

*Opaekaa Falls*

*Wailua River*

# KUAMOO–NOUNOU TRAIL
## (TO VALLEY VISTA HALE)

# Hike 31
## Kuamoo—Nounou Trail to Nounou Mountain Trail West "Sleeping Giant"

**Hiking distance:** 3.6 miles round trip
**Hiking time:** 2 hours
**Elevation gain:** 400 feet
**Maps:** U.S.G.S. Kapaa
Recreational Map of Eastern Kauai

**Summary of hike:** The Kuamoo-Nounou Trail is one of three access trails leading up to the summit of Nounou Mountain, known as the Sleeping Giant. This route follows the southern access through the forest reserve along a cliffside shelf on the west side of the mountain. The forested trail offers picturesque views of Mount Waialeale, Kawaikini and the Makaleha Mountains.

**Driving directions:** From Lihue, drive six miles north on Highway 56 to Kuamoo Road/Highway 580, the first intersection after crossing the Wailua River. Turn left and continue 2.4 miles to the parking area on the right. The parking area is 0.7 miles past Opaekaa Falls, directly across from Nelia Street.

**Hiking directions:** Follow the hiking directions of Hike 30 to Valley Vista Hale, the picnic shelter and overlook. From the shelter, hike northeast, contouring along the west flank of Nounou Mountain under the dense forest canopy. The path parallels the forest reserve boundary with frequent dips and rises, passing groves of guava, eucalyptus and Norfolk Island pines. Near the end of the trail, gently descend to a junction with the Nounou Mountain Trail West at 1.8 miles. This is the resting and turnaround point for this hike. Return on the same trail.

To hike further, the Nounou Mountain Trail West (Hike 29) continues to the right through a lane bordered by two parallel rows of Norfolk Island pines. The trail climbs 1.5 miles up to Alii Vista Hale at the summit.

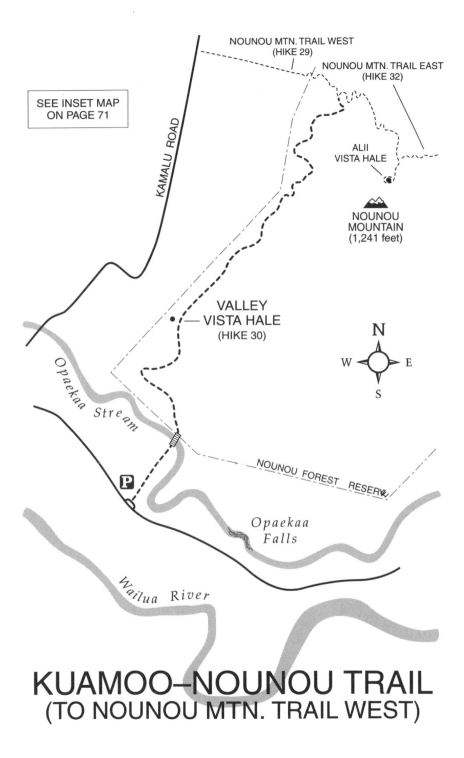

NOUNOU MTN. TRAIL WEST
(HIKE 29)

NOUNOU MTN. TRAIL EAST
(HIKE 32)

ALII
VISTA HALE

NOUNOU
MOUNTAIN
(1,241 feet)

SEE INSET MAP
ON PAGE 71

KAMALU ROAD

VALLEY
VISTA HALE
(HIKE 30)

N
W   E
S

Opaekaa Stream

P

NOUNOU FOREST RESERVE

Opaekaa
Falls

Wailua River

# KUAMOO–NOUNOU TRAIL
## (TO NOUNOU MTN. TRAIL WEST)

# Hike 32
# Nounou Mountain Trail East to Alii Vista Hale
## "Sleeping Giant"

**Hiking distance:** 3.5 miles round trip
**Hiking time:** 2 hours
**Elevation gain:** 1,000 feet
**Maps:** U.S.G.S. Kapaa
       Recreational Map of Eastern Kauai

**Summary of hike:** The Nounou Mountain Trail East is one of the three trails that climbs up to the summit of Nounou Mountain, also known as Sleeping Giant. The trail follows the eastern access up a series of switchbacks through the forest. The path ends at Alii Vista Hale, a picnic shelter at the summit on the chest of the giant. Along the way are spectacular views of the Wailua River and the seacoast communities from Anahola to Lihue. From Alii Vista Hale are views to the west of the cloud-engulfed Mount Waialeale in the Makaleha Mountains, the headwaters for all seven major rivers on Kauai.

**Driving directions:** From Lihue, drive 6 miles north on Highway 56 to Haleilio Road, the second intersection after crossing the Wailua River. Turn left and continue 1.1 mile to the Nounou Mountain East trailhead parking lot on the right.

**Hiking directions:** The trail begins on the right side of the parking lot to the right of the rock wall. The path immediately enters the lush forest. Switchbacks allow for a gradual and easy ascent. At 0.7 miles, the path descends for a short distance, then regains the climb, passing numerous overlooks. The path crosses over to the west side of the ridge and back to the east a couple of times as it nears the top. Views alternate between the mountainous interior and the eastern coastline. The trail reaches a 3-way junction at 1.7 miles. The Nounou Mountain Trail West (Hike 29) bears to the right. Take the left fork a short distance to Alii Vista Hale, a picnic shelter on a flat, grassy knoll. After enjoying the summit, return along the same path.

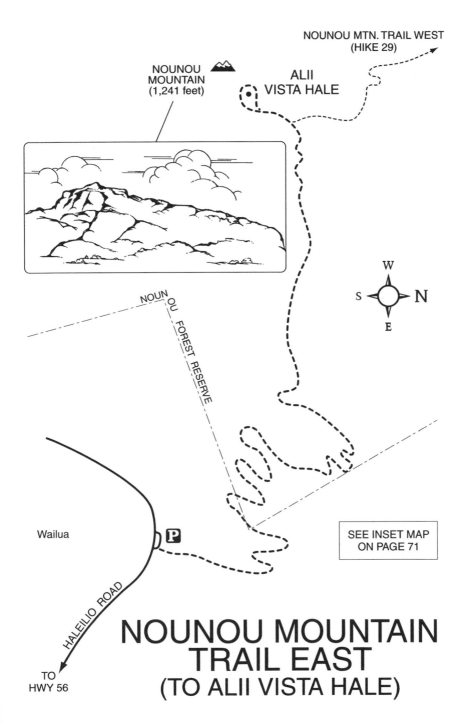

NOUNOU MTN. TRAIL WEST
(HIKE 29)

NOUNOU
MOUNTAIN
(1,241 feet)

ALII
VISTA HALE

W

S ✦ N

E

NOUNOU FOREST RESERVE

Wailua

🅿

SEE INSET MAP
ON PAGE 71

HALEILIO ROAD

TO
HWY 56

# NOUNOU MOUNTAIN
# TRAIL EAST
## (TO ALII VISTA HALE)

# Hike 33
# North Kapaa Ocean Walk
# to Kealia Lookout

**Hiking distance:** 2 miles round trip
**Hiking time:** 1 hour
**Elevation gain:** 50 feet
**Maps:** U.S.G.S. Kapaa
        Recreation Map of Eastern Kauai

**Summary of hike:** This hike takes you along an old abandoned road perched above the ocean. The road, well hidden from the highway, was an old cane hauling route. The views along this rugged coastline are magnificent. A side trail leads up to Kealia Lookout, a grassy knoll and overlook with panoramic views up and down the jagged coastline.

**Driving directions:** From Lihue, drive 9 miles north on Highway 56 to the north end of Kapaa. Park in the pullout on the right (ocean) side of the road by mile marker 9. The pullout is across the road from Kapaa Jodo Mission at Hauaala Road.

**Hiking directions:** From the parking pullout, walk south 50 feet to the old road. Head northeast, following the ridge above the ocean. Along the way, various side paths lead down to the sandy beach. Near the far end of the road, at 0.8 miles, is a large knoll—Kealia Lookout. To the right, paths lead down to the ocean and up to the top of the knoll. From the summit are coastal views from Kealia Beach and Paliku Point in the north to Kapaa Beach in the south. At one mile, the trail rejoins Highway 56 by the Kapaa Stream bridge adjacent to Kealia Beach. Return to your car along the same path.

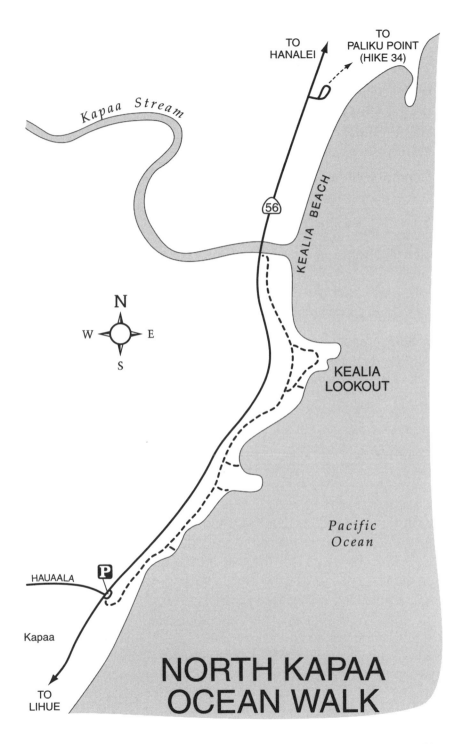

TO
HANALEI

TO
PALIKU POINT
(HIKE 34)

*Kapaa Stream*

56

KEALIA BEACH

N

W    E

S

KEALIA
LOOKOUT

*Pacific
Ocean*

HAUAALA

P

Kapaa

TO
LIHUE

# NORTH KAPAA
# OCEAN WALK

# Hike 34
# Kealia Cliffside Trail

**Hiking distance:** 2.4 miles round trip
**Hiking time:** 1.5 hours
**Elevation gain:** 50 feet
**Maps:** U.S.G.S. Kapaa

**Summary of hike:** Kealia Beach is a popular surfing beach bordered by rocky points. Kapaa Stream flows across the south end of the beach. At the north end is a sheltered cove protected by a jetty. The cliffside trail is an old cane hauling road that begins at the north end of this beach near the shore-break. The graded, red dirt road overlooks the sea while following the edge of the cliffs to Paliku Point. From the point are dramatic coastal views.

**Driving directions:** From Lihue, drive 10.5 miles north on Highway 56 to the parking lot at the north end of Kealia Beach between mile markers 10 and 11. Turn right and park.

**Hiking directions:** Rather than following the shoreline, take the rock-lined road at the north end of the parking lot above the sandy beach. Head north towards the cliffs, parallel to the ocean. The path is perched on the hillside above the tidepools and crashing waves. At one mile, as you round the first point, is a trail split. Stay to the right, following close to the ocean. A short distance ahead, large boulders have been placed across the path where there was once a bridge. Take the footpath on the left across the ravine. The path returns back to the main trail on the red dirt road. To the right, a short detour leads to huge rock formations at the ocean bluffs and an old concrete platform jutting out to sea, once used as a pineapple loading pier. Return to the trail and continue north, reaching Paliku Point at 1.2 miles. Leave the road and explore the point and the magnificent views. To return, retrace your steps.

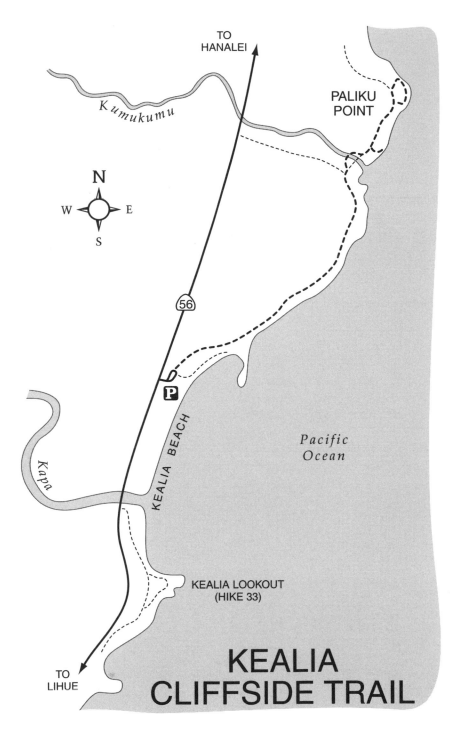

TO
HANALEI

*Kumukumu*

N
W   E
S

(56)

PALIKU
POINT

KEALIA BEACH

*Kapa*

*Pacific
Ocean*

P

KEALIA LOOKOUT
(HIKE 33)

TO
LIHUE

# KEALIA
# CLIFFSIDE TRAIL

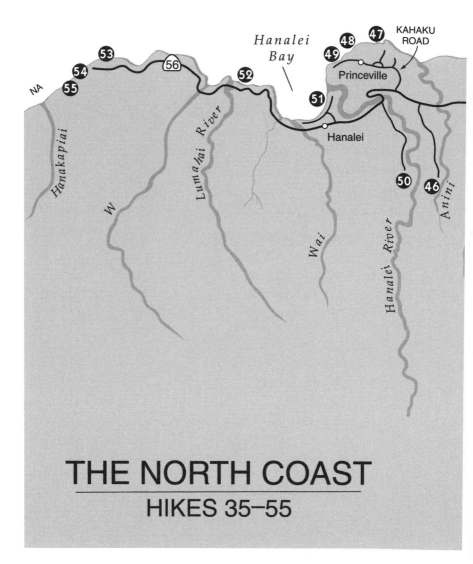

Pacific Ocean

Hanalei Bay

KAHAKU ROAD

Princeville

NA

Hanakapiai

W

Lumahai River

Hanalei

Wai

Hanalei River

Anini

# THE NORTH COAST
## HIKES 35–55

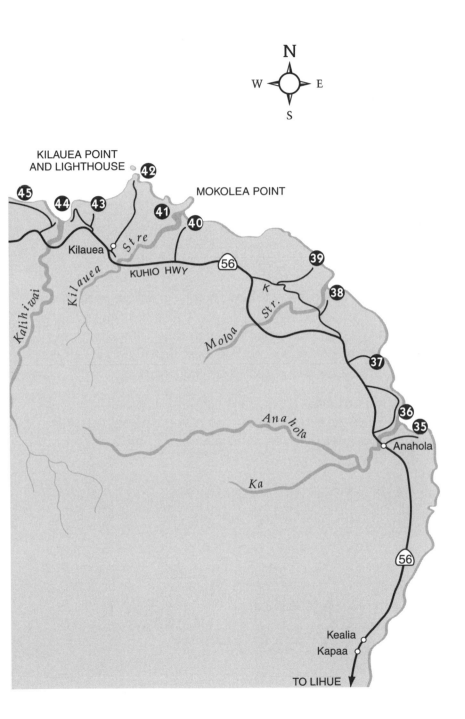

KILAUEA POINT
AND LIGHTHOUSE

MOKOLEA POINT

KILAUEA POINT
AND LIGHTHOUSE

N
W ← → E
S

45

44    43

42

41

40

39

38

37

36
35

Kilauea

KUHIO  HWY

56

Kilauea  Str e

Kalihiwai

Kilauea

Moloa

K Str.

Anahola

Ka

Anahola

56

Kealia

Kapaa

TO LIHUE

# Hike 35
# Anahola Beach
# Kahala Point to Anahola Stream

**Hiking distance:** 1.2 miles round trip
**Hiking time:** 1 hour
**Elevation gain:** Level
**Maps:** U.S.G.S. Anahola
　　　　　Recreation Map of Eastern Kauai

**Summary of hike:** Anahola Beach is a long, wide sandy beach on the south side of Anahola Bay. The bay, bordered by Kahala Point and Kuaehu Point, lies in a protected cove with a large offshore reef. Anahola Stream flows down from the inland mountains and divides the bay, separating Anahola Beach from Aliomanu Beach (Hike 36). Along the stream are large shallow pools. This beachside path travels through Anahola Beach County Park, a neighborhood park with a flat, grassy camping area in a shady ironwood and hau tree grove. The park has showers, restrooms, picnic tables and barbecues.

**Driving directions:** From Lihue, drive 13.5 miles north on Highway 56 to Anahola Road between mile markers 13 and 14. Turn right and drive 0.8 miles to a parking lot at the east end of the bay. Turn left and park.

**Hiking directions:** Walk out to the oceanfront by the old cement pier pilings. Head east (right), following the sandy shoreline or the grassy, tree-lined path towards Kahala Point at the east end of the bay. The path ends near black lava rocks at the base of the bluffs. Heading back west, stroll along the shoreline to the mouth of Anahola Stream and a lagoon. When the stream is low, wade across to Aliomanu Beach (Hike 36), and continue north to Kuaehu Point. Return the way you came.

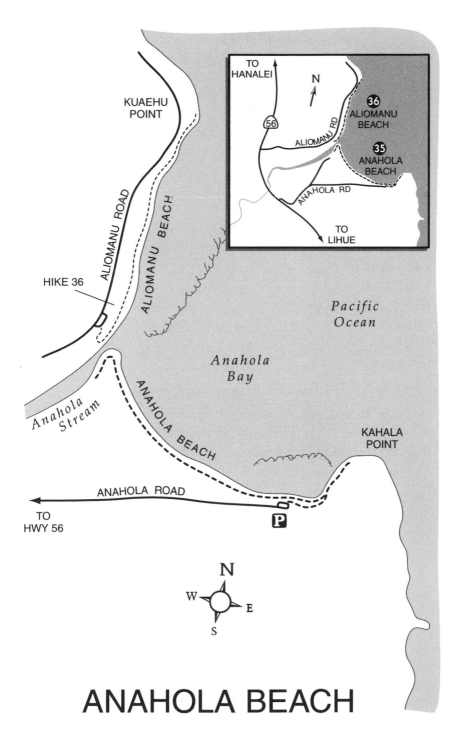

KUAEHU
POINT

HIKE 36

TO
HANALEI

N

56

ALIOMANU RD

36
ALIOMANU
BEACH

ALIOMANU

35
ANAHOLA
BEACH

ANAHOLA RD

TO
LIHUE

ALIOMANU ROAD

ALIOMANU BEACH

*Pacific
Ocean*

*Anahola
Bay*

*Anahola
Stream*

ANAHOLA BEACH

KAHALA
POINT

ANAHOLA  ROAD

TO
HWY 56

P

N
W        E
S

# ANAHOLA BEACH

# Hike 36
# Aliomanu Beach

**Hiking distance:** 1.2 miles round trip
**Hiking time:** 1 hour
**Elevation gain:** Level
**Maps:** U.S.G.S. Anahola
         Recreation Map of Eastern Kauai

**Summary of hike:** This hike is an easy, meandering beach stroll on a narrow, tree-lined ribbon of sand along Anahola Bay. The half-mile stretch is bordered to the north by Kuaehu Point and to the south by Anahola Stream and a lagoon. Near the stream is a picnic area with tables in a shady grove of ironwood and kamani trees. The beach has an extensive offshore reef and is a popular fishing spot for locals. The views extend across Anahola Beach (Hike 35) to Kahala Point at the east tip of the bay. This walk may be combined with Hike 35 when Anahola Stream is low.

**Driving directions:** From Lihue, drive 14 miles north on Highway 56 to Aliomanu Road, just beyond mile marker 14. Turn right and drive 0.6 miles to the parking area at the south end of the beach, adjacent to Anahola Stream. Park on the right under the grove of ironwood trees.

**Hiking directions:** Walk through the shady picnic area along Anahola Stream and the lagoon. From the mouth of the stream, follow the sandy shoreline north, passing several beachside houses. At 0.6 miles, the strand reaches Kuaehu Point by a pile of black boulders at the north tip of the bay. This is our turn-around spot.

When the stream is low, wade across Anahola Stream to Anahola Beach. You may continue your hike to Kahala Point (Hike 35).

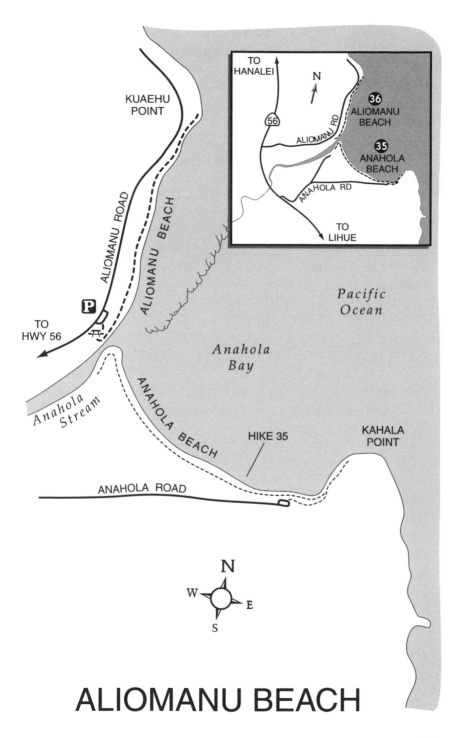

KUAEHU
POINT

TO
HANALEI

N

56

ALIOMANU RD

ALIOMANU

36
ALIOMANU
BEACH

35
ANAHOLA
BEACH

ANAHOLA RD

TO
LIHUE

ALIOMANU ROAD

ALIOMANU BEACH

P

TO
HWY 56

*Pacific
Ocean*

*Anahola
Bay*

*Anahola
Stream*

ANAHOLA BEACH

HIKE 35

KAHALA
POINT

ANAHOLA ROAD

N

W        E

S

# ALIOMANU BEACH

# Hike 37
# Papaa Bay

**Hiking distance:** 1 mile round trip
**Hiking time:** 1 hour
**Elevation gain:** 160 feet
**Maps:** U.S.G.S. Anahola
Recreation Map of Eastern Kauai

**Summary of hike:** Papaa Bay is a small coral-lined bay tucked into the high sea cliffs northwest of Anahola. Shallow reefs fringe the beautiful crescent-shaped beach. An access road leads to the top of the 160-foot sea cliffs above Papaa Bay, where this trail descends off the bluffs to the tropical shoreline at the south end of the bay.

**Driving directions:** From Lihue, drive 15.5 miles north on Highway 56 to Papaa Road, between mile markers 15 and 16, and turn right. Drive a quarter mile to a road junction and turn right. Go 0.2 miles and turn left, following the "beach access" signs. Continue 0.3 miles to a signed junction and turn right. Drive into the trailhead parking lot 0.1 mile ahead.

**Hiking directions:** Walk through the trailhead gate, and bear left on the red dirt trail. Follow the hilltop toward the ocean. At the edge of the bluffs, curve right and begin the descent on the rough unpaved road into the ravine. The trail drops onto the sand at the mouth of the ravine. To the right, follow the south edge of the isolated bay along the narrow, forest-lined strand. Views extend south to Kahala Point by Anahola Bay. To the left, the path crosses lava rocks jutting out to sea.

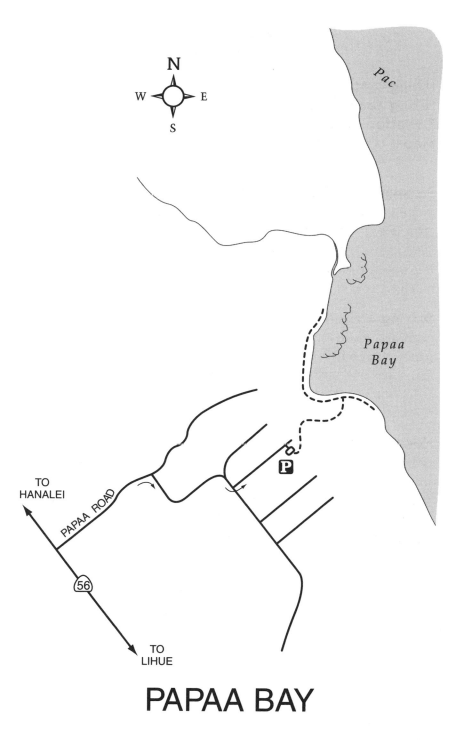

# PAPAA BAY

# Hike 38
# Moloaa Bay

**Hiking distance:** 1.5 miles round trip
**Hiking time:** 1 hour
**Elevation gain:** Level
**Maps:** U.S.G.S. Anahola
         Recreation Map of Eastern Kauai

**Summary of hike:** Moloaa Bay is a secluded horseshoe-shaped bay enclosed on each side by high bluffs. The wide crescent of sand terminates on each end at the forested hillsides. Moloaa Stream flows across the golden strand, dividing the bay. The beach is backed by groves of ironwood, paper mulberry and heliotrope trees.

**Driving directions:** From Lihue, drive 16.5 miles north on Highway 56 to the first Koolau Road turnoff between mile markers 16 and 17. Turn right and drive 1.2 miles to Moloaa Road. Turn right again and continue 0.8 miles, bearing left at a road fork. Head to the parking area on the left near the end of the road.

**Hiking directions:** Walk to the end of the road to the designated beach accesses on each side of the last house. Walk through the gate at the end of the road, dropping onto the sand by Moloaa Stream. Wade across the shallow stream, heading northeast towards Ka Lae Amana. A forested path along the base of the hills also parallels the shoreline. The sandy beach ends at a pile of black lava rocks by the hills of Ka Lae Amana. Return and recross Moloaa Stream to the south end of the bay. Continue southeast, crossing a concrete slab to the sheltered side of the bay. A half mile ahead, a pile of boulders at the base of the sheer, forested bluffs prevents further travel.

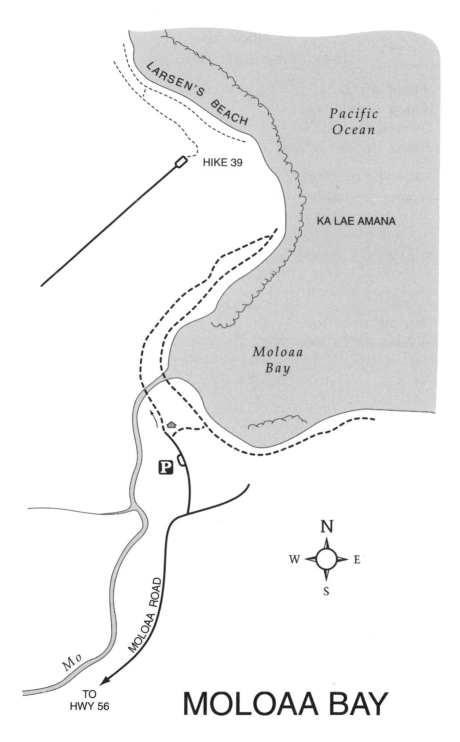

LARSEN'S BEACH

*Pacific Ocean*

HIKE 39

KA LAE AMANA

*Moloaa Bay*

P

MOLOAA ROAD

*Mo*

TO HWY 56

N
W E
S

# MOLOAA BAY

# Hike 39
# Kaakaaniu "Larsen's" Beach

**Hiking distance:** 1.5 miles round trip
**Hiking time:** 1 hour
**Elevation gain:** 200 feet
**Maps:** U.S.G.S. Anahola

**Summary of hike:** Kaakaaniu Beach, known locally as Larsen's Beach, is a long, narrow beach between Kulikoa and Ka Lae Amana Points. The secluded beach sits at the base of low rolling hills and is backed by sand dunes with small trees, scrub and walking paths. A gently sloping path leads down from the bluffs to the beach. There are several rustic shacks used by local fisherman. Larsen's beach is an excellent snorkeling site with clear, shallow water and a wide fringing reef.

**Driving directions:** From Lihue, drive 16.5 miles north on Highway 56 to the first Koolau Road turnoff between mile markers 16 and 17. Turn right and drive 2.3 miles to a road on the right. Turn sharply to the right. Follow the beach access road past horse pastures for 0.9 miles to the trailhead parking area at the end of the road.

**Hiking directions:** Walk through the beach access gate, and follow the wide dirt path 200 feet above the ocean. The path curves northwest, gradually descending towards the beach to a trail fork. The right fork drops down to the beach—our return route. Continue straight on the left fork, following the rolling hillsides parallel to the coastline. At 0.6 miles, the path ends at a fenced property line just shy of Pakala Point, a low rocky point. Take an access route to the shoreline, and head back along the sand. Pass occasional rock outcroppings along the shore. Continue past the return access to a pile of lava rocks along the north edge of Ka Lae Amana, where the hillside drops into the sea. Head back to the return access and up to the parking area.

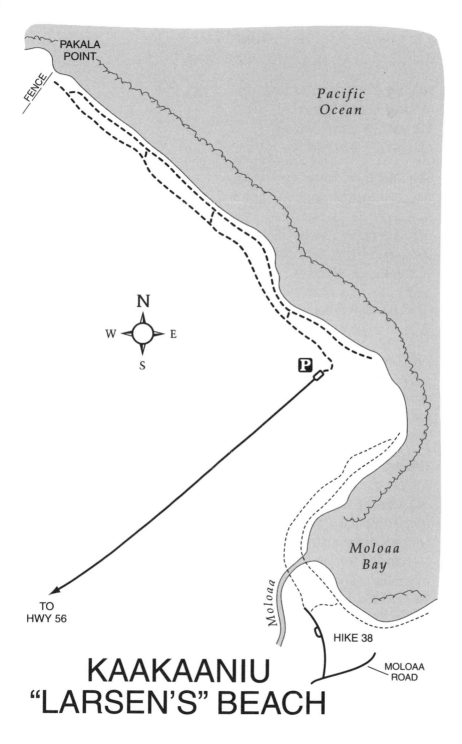

PAKALA
POINT

FENCE

*Pacific
Ocean*

N
W E
S

P

TO
HWY 56

*Moloaa
Bay*

*Moloaa*

HIKE 38

MOLOAA
ROAD

# KAAKAANIU
# "LARSEN'S" BEACH

# Hike 40
# Kilauea Bay

**Hiking distance:** 1.2 miles round trip
**Hiking time:** 1 hour
**Elevation gain:** 100 feet
**Maps:** U.S.G.S. Anahola

**Summary of hike:** Kilauea Bay is a picturesque half-moon bay between two tree-covered rocky bluffs. Kahili Quarry Beach sits in this secluded cove fringed with groves of ironwood trees. Windswept cliffs line the east side of the bay. At the base of the cliffs are tidepools in the pile of lava rocks. Kilauea Stream and a lagoon border the western edge of the beach. Just past the mouth of the stream, the rock formations of Mokolea Point extend out to sea. The peninsula is part of the 160-acre Kilauea National Wildlife Refuge.

**Driving directions:** From Lihue, drive 21.5 miles north and west on Highway 56 to Wailapa Road between mile markers 21 and 22. Turn right and drive a half mile to an unpaved road on the left. Turn left and descend 0.6 miles, overlooking the Kilauea Stream, to an unimproved parking area at the end of the road.

**Hiking directions:** To the right, a short red dirt path leads through the forest to a grassy knoll overlooking the bay. To the left, take the two-track trail parallel to the bay through the lush forest. Several side paths lead down to the beach on the right. The main path winds through ironwood groves to Kilauea Stream and the lagoon at the mouth of the river. After enjoying this area, return along the beach. At the east end of the bay, the sand terminates at the cliffs by lava rocks and tidepools.

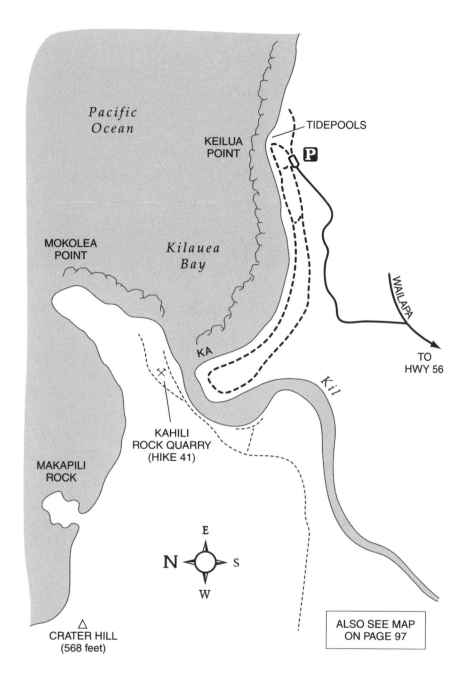

Pacific
Ocean

KEILUA
POINT

TIDEPOOLS

**P**

MOKOLEA
POINT

*Kilauea
Bay*

WAILAPA

KA

TO
HWY 56

*Kil*

KAHILI
ROCK QUARRY
(HIKE 41)

MAKAPILI
ROCK

E

N ○ S

W

ALSO SEE MAP
ON PAGE 97

△
CRATER HILL
(568 feet)

# KILAUEA BAY

# Hike 41
# Kahili Rock Quarry

**Hiking distance:** 3 miles round trip
**Hiking time:** 1.5 hours
**Elevation gain:** 300 feet
**Maps:** U.S.G.S. Anahola

**Summary of hike:** Kahili Rock Quarry sits along the rugged cliffs of Mokolea Point, part of the Kilauea National Wildlife Refuge. The abandoned rock quarry overlooks the crescent-shaped Kilauea Bay from above Kilauea Stream and the blue Pacific. The views extend across the bay, which is rimmed by groves of ironwood trees, to the forested windswept cliffs along the bay's eastern edge. The hike follows an old rutted road to the ocean to the quarry and an overlook.

**Driving directions:** From Lihue, drive 23.5 miles north on Highway 56 to the town of Kilauea. Turn right on Kolo Road, located between mile markers 23 and 24. Drive one block and turn left on Kilauea Road. Continue 0.7 miles through town to a dirt road on the right. Park along the right side of the road by the metal gate.

**Hiking directions:** Follow the unpaved road east along a row of mature ironwood trees teeming with the sounds of birds. At a half mile, the road begins a gradual descent past a banana orchard on the left. Kilauea Stream can be seen down in the river valley to the right. As the path curves left, views open up to the ocean and the lagoon at the mouth of the stream in Kilauea Bay. Near the bay is a trail fork. The right fork leads down to a flat grassy grove at the edge of the stream. The sandy cove across the stream is fringed with groves of ironwood trees. The main trail continues straight, following the west edge of the bay towards Mokolea Point. Climb up the rocky road by the old quarry to a scenic overlook. Views extend across the bay to Keilua Point and Kepuhi Point farther east. Access is not allowed to Mokolea Point.

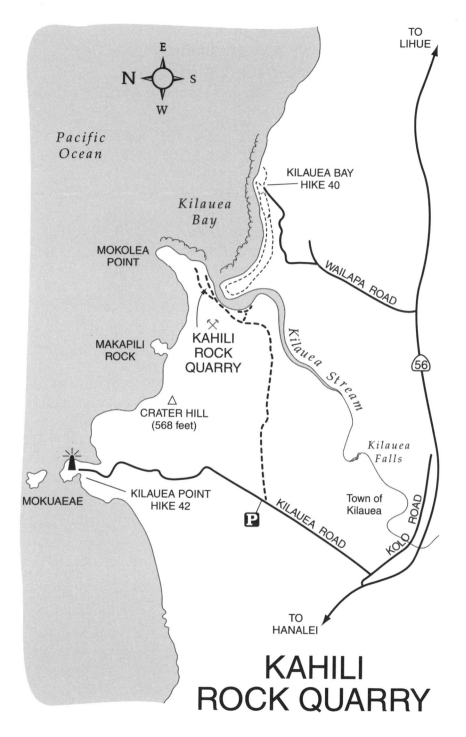

# KAHILI
# ROCK QUARRY

# Hike 42
# Kilauea Point National Wildlife Refuge and Kilauea Lighthouse

OPEN MONDAY—FRIDAY · 10 A.M.—4 P.M.

**Hiking distance:** 0.3 miles round trip
**Hiking time:** 1 hour
**Elevation gain:** Level
**Maps:** U.S.G.S. Anahola
Recreation Map of Eastern Kauai

**Summary of hike:** Kilauea Point National Wildlife Refuge and the historic Kilauea Lighthouse are located at the northernmost point in Kauai as well as the major Hawaiian Islands. This short, self-guided path on the 160-acre refuge follows the perimeter of the peninsula 200 feet above the sea. The point has breathtaking views of chiseled coastal cliffs, the crashing surf and a picturesque lighthouse built in 1913 perched on the bluff. The trail overlooks the island of Mokuaeae, a sanctuary for thousands of nesting and migratory birds, including Laysan albatross, wedge-tailed shearwaters and red-footed boobies. Kilauea Point also offers an opportunity to observe seals, dolphins, sea turtles and seasonal humpback whales from December through April.

**Driving directions:** From Lihue, drive 23.5 miles north on Highway 56 to the town of Kilauea. Turn right on Kolo Road, located between mile markers 23 and 24. Drive one block and turn left on Kilauea Road. Continue 1.6 miles to the end of the road. Turn left to the wildlife refuge entrance. The parking lot is a short distance ahead.

**Hiking directions:** From the parking area, walk towards the lighthouse to the north tip of the peninsula. Stroll around the fenced perimeter overlooking the sheer rugged cliffs of Mokolea Point (Hike 41), the island of Mokuaeae, and Crater Hill, a remnant of an eroded tuff cone, all part of the refuge.

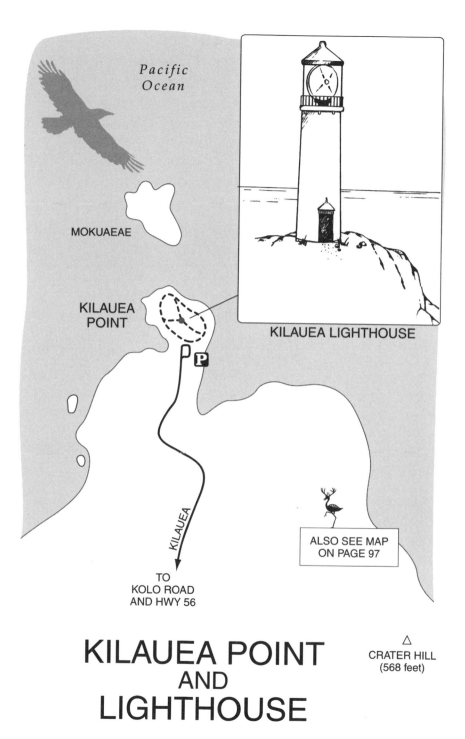

Pacific
Ocean

MOKUAEAE

KILAUEA
POINT

**P**

KILAUEA LIGHTHOUSE

KILAUEA

ALSO SEE MAP
ON PAGE 97

TO
KOLO ROAD
AND HWY 56

# KILAUEA POINT
## AND
# LIGHTHOUSE

△
CRATER HILL
(568 feet)

# Hike 43
# Kauapea "Secret" Beach

**Hiking distance:** 2 mile round trip
**Hiking time:** 1.5 hours
**Elevation gain:** 200 feet
**Maps:** U.S.G.S. Anahola and Hanalei

**Summary of hike:** Kauapea Beach, known locally as Secret Beach, is a long secluded stretch of golden sand at the base of the sheer cliffs just west of Kilauea Point. It is unofficially a clothing optional beach. From the beach are great views of the Kilauea Lighthouse and the island of Mokuaeae, a sanctuary for thousands of nesting and migratory birds (Hike 42). The access is down a ravine through a tropical forest with palms and hanging vines to the base of the cliffs.

**Driving directions:** From Lihue, drive 24.5 miles north and west on Highway 56 to the first Kalihiwai Road on the right between mile markers 24 and 25. Turn right and drive 0.1 mile to an unpaved road on the right. Turn right and continue 0.4 miles to the parking area at the end of the road.

**Hiking directions:** Walk down the clearly defined trail under the shade of a forest canopy. Follow the fenceline along the edge of the cliffs overlooking the deep ravine. Descend into the jungle, zigzagging along the east-facing hillside on root, rock and dirt steps. At the base of the ravine, the trail emerges from the forest onto the sandy beach. On the left, towards Kapukaamoi Point, slabs of lava rock can be crossed to tidepools near the crashing surf. To the right, follow the shoreline along the base of the forested cliffs past small caves. The path ends where the cliffs of Kilauea Point meet the sea.

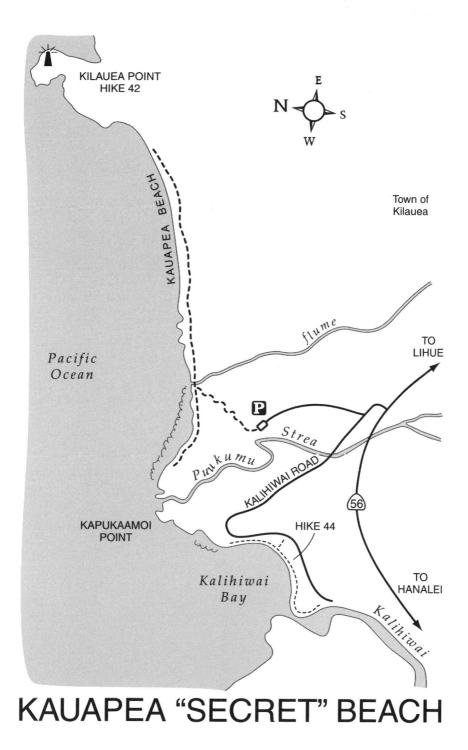

# KAUAPEA "SECRET" BEACH

# Hike 44
## Kalihiwai Bay

**Hiking distance:** 1 mile round trip
**Hiking time:** 30 minutes
**Elevation gain:** Level
**Maps:** U.S.G.S. Hanalei
       Recreational Map of Eastern Kauai

**Summary of hike:** Kalihiwai Bay is a deep water bay with a wide crescent of sand. The bay is rimmed by shady groves of ironwood trees and picnic tables. The sheer rock lava cliffs of Ka Lae O Kowali on the west and the towering sea cliffs of Kapukaamoi Point on the east border each side of the protected bay. The Kalihiwai River flows out of the interior valley, crossing the center of the pristine bay en route to the sea. At the mouth of the river is a large, shallow lagoon.

**Driving directions:** From Lihue, drive 24.5 miles north and west on Highway 56 to the first Kalihiwai Road on the right between mile markers 24 and 25. Turn right and drive 1.2 miles downhill to the center of Kalihiwai Bay. Park on the right under a grove of mature ironwood trees.

**Hiking directions:** From the parking area, walk along the beach to the left (west) on the firm sand. The path leads to the wide mouth of the Kalihiwai River at the southern end of the picturesque bay. Across the river are magnificent views of the lush forested hillsides. Return to the right along the wide, curved pocket of the bay parallel to the ironwood trees on the backshore. The beach strand ends at the base of black lava rock formations extending out to sea.

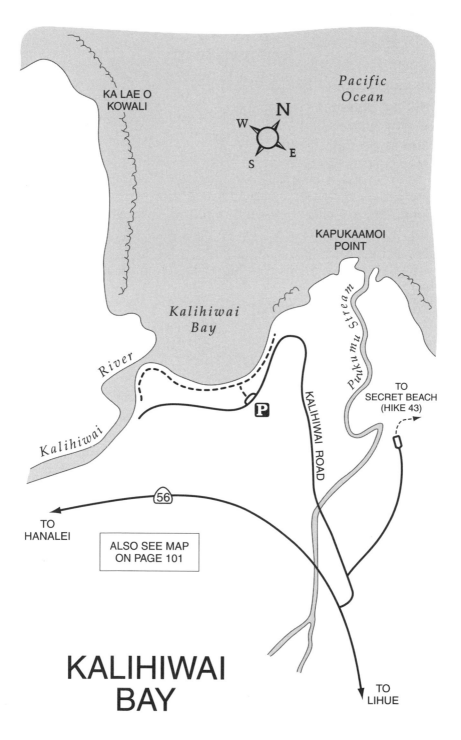

KA LAE O
KOWALI

*Pacific
Ocean*

N
W      E
S

KAPUKAAMOI
POINT

*Kalihiwai
Bay*

*Pukumu Stream*

*River*

*Kalihiwai*

P

TO
SECRET BEACH
(HIKE 43)

KALIHIWAI ROAD

56

TO
HANALEI

ALSO SEE MAP
ON PAGE 101

TO
LIHUE

# KALIHIWAI
BAY

# Hike 45
## Kalihikai Beach
## Anini Beach County Park

**Hiking distance:** 2 miles round trip
**Hiking time:** 1 hour
**Elevation gain:** Level
**Maps:** U.S.G.S. Hanalei
       Recreation Map of Eastern Kauai

**Summary of hike:** Kalihikai Beach (the same as Anini Beach County Park) is a 12-acre park fronting the beautiful Pacific. It has a tree-lined grassy picnic area with tables, restrooms, showers and barbecue grills. The beach is a popular windsurfing and snorkeling spot with lagoons protected by fringing reefs. At the west end of the Kalihikai Beach (Anini Beach County Park) are the black rock cliffs of Honu Point and Honono Point. Beyond Honono Point is Anini Beach, an undeveloped beach strand that is usually deserted.

**Driving directions:** From Lihue, drive 25.5 miles north and west on Highway 56 to the second Kalihiwai Bay turnoff between mile markers 25 and 26. It is located 0.3 miles past a large bridge over the Kalihiwai River. Turn right on Kalihiwai Road, and drive a quarter mile to a road fork. Bear left on the Anini Road, and continue 1.4 miles, descending to the beachfront at Anini Beach County Park on the right.

**Hiking directions:** From the east end of Kalihikai Beach, bear left along the sandy beach, or take the shady grass strip through the groves of kamani, almond, heliotrope and ironwood trees. At the west end of the flat, near Honu Point, are campsites. For additional hiking, drive a short distance west past Honono Point to numerous parking pullouts. Beachcomb along the various coves of Anini Beach into the tree-lined bay.

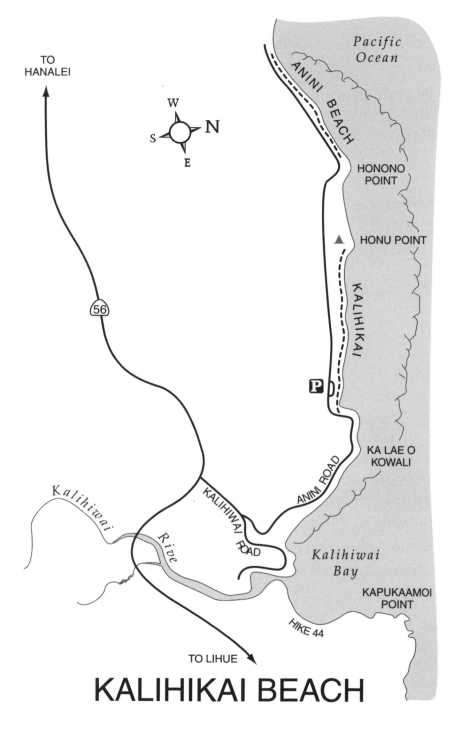

# KALIHIKAI BEACH

# Hike 46
# Powerline Trail
# (northern access)

**Hiking distance:** 2.5 miles round trip
**Hiking time:** 1 hour
**Elevation gain:** 200 feet
**Maps:** U.S.G.S. Hanalei
　　　　Recreation Map of Eastern Kauai

**Summary of hike:** The Powerline Trail is a 10.5-mile trail through the interior mountain valleys, linking the north shore with the east side of the island. The trail is a red dirt road that follows powerlines through the forest reserve. This short hike starts at the trail's northern access and follows the first mile of the muddy dirt road. The trail travels above the Hanalei Valley, overlooking the river, Hanalei National Wildlife Refuge and the ocean beyond Hanalei Bay. Through openings in the lush foliage, waterfalls can be seen falling off faraway cliffs. For a strenuous all-day experience, this trail can be combined with Hike 24 (the southern access route) for a fantastic one-way shuttle hike.

**Driving directions:** From Lihue, drive 27 miles north and west on Highway 56 to Pooku Road, located after mile marker 27. The turnoff is about a mile past the Princeville Airport by the horse stables. Turn left (south) and drive 1.9 miles to the trailhead parking area on the left, past the water tank by the hunters' check-in box. The last 0.2 miles are unpaved.

**Hiking directions:** Walk south on the red clay road lined with lush tropical vegetation. A side trail merges from the right at 0.2 miles. Continue gently uphill on several small dips and rises. At a half mile, views open up to the Hanalei National Wildlife Refuge and the Hanalei River on the right (west). As you approach the one-mile mark, which lies across the valley from the triangular-shaped peak of Hihimanu, watch for openings in the dense foliage. The views across the agricultural valley include numerous waterfalls dropping hundreds of feet off the sheer cliffs of the mountains. This is our turnaround spot.

To hike further, the next few miles follow a gentle grade with numerous ups and downs, skirting the west flank of Kapaka above the Kalihiwai River.

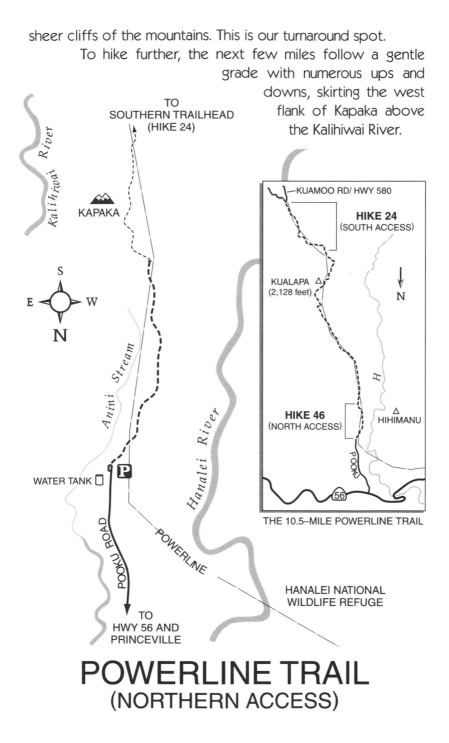

THE 10.5–MILE POWERLINE TRAIL

# POWERLINE TRAIL
## (NORTHERN ACCESS)

# Hike 47
## "Sea Lodge Beach"
## Kaweonui Beach

**Hiking distance:** 1 mile round trip
**Hiking time:** 1 hour
**Elevation gain:** 150 feet
**Maps:** U.S.G.S. Hanalei

**Summary of hike:** Sea Lodge Beach is a secluded beach at the base of the steep sea cliffs in Princeville. The small, protected cove is tucked into an indentation at the base of steep green cliffs. The trail winds through a tropical jungle to the sea at Kaweonui Point.

**Driving directions:** From Lihue, drive 28 miles north and west on Highway 56 to Kahaku Road at the Princeville sign, just before the Princeville Shopping Center. Turn right and drive 0.9 miles to Pepelani Road. Turn right and go 0.2 miles to Kaweonui Road. Turn right again and drive 0.4 miles to Keoniana Road. Turn right and park along the side of the road. (See inset map on page 113.)

**Hiking directions:** Walk 30 yards down Keoniana Road to a long paved driveway on the right. Bear right and head east past the gate on the service road. Walk downhill through the forest, and cross over a seasonal stream to the end of the road at a fenced pump installation. Take the left fork on the footpath along the right side of the stream to a trail split. The right fork leads to an overlook on the bluffs behind the Sea Cliff Hotel. Take the left fork down a few steps and across the stream. The jungle path winds downhill through lush vegetation. The trail is wet and precarious, demanding full concentration. Continue down a long series of gravel steps to the coast at Kaweonui Point. Curve left and watch for a short detour on the right to a lookout on Kaweonui Point, a black lava rock shelf. On the main trail continue west, curving into Sea Lodge Beach. The small pocket of sand is nestled at the base of the 150-foot cliffs.

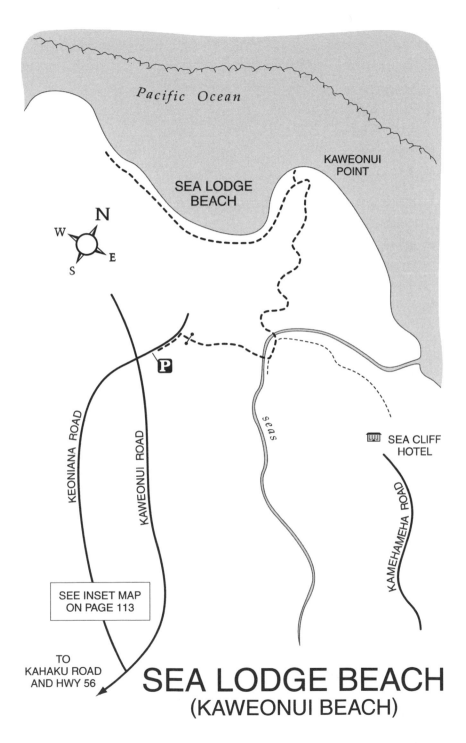

Pacific Ocean

KAWEONUI POINT

SEA LODGE BEACH

N
W E
S

P

KEONIANA ROAD

KAWEONUI ROAD

KAMEHAMEHA ROAD

seas

SEA CLIFF HOTEL

SEE INSET MAP ON PAGE 113

TO KAHAKU ROAD AND HWY 56

# SEA LODGE BEACH
## (KAWEONUI BEACH)

# Hike 48
# Queen's Bath

**Hiking distance:** 0.6 miles round trip
**Hiking time:** 30 minutes
**Elevation gain:** 150 feet
**Maps:** U.S.G.S. Hanalei

**Summary of hike:** Queen's Bath is a natural pool carved into the lava shelf at the base of the cliffs in Princeville. An inlet connects the pool to the ocean. Queen's Bath constantly changes due to the time of year, surf and tides. During the winter, the bath may not be easy to identify due to the pounding surf. From the lava shelf and pool are beautiful mountain and coastal views. The trail parallels a stream past a freshwater waterfall and pool. There are steep inclines, loose footing and narrow ledges. Use caution and good judgement while negotiating this path.

**Driving directions:** From Lihue, drive 28 miles north and west on Highway 56 to Kahaku Road at the Princeville sign, just before the Princeville Shopping Center. Turn right and drive 1.4 miles to Punahele Road and turn right. Continue 0.3 miles to the second Kapiolani Road intersection and turn right. Park in the signed parking lot on the left. (See inset map on page 113.)

**Hiking directions:** Take the well-defined path, past the caution signs, on the right side of the parking lot. Descend into the lush, shady forest. Tree roots on the trail are helpful for better footholds. Along the way, the path begins paralleling a stream on the right to the top of a waterfall and pool. Descend a short distance to a spur trail on the right leading to the pool at the base of the falls. Return to the main trail and continue downhill, following the stream towards the ocean. The path emerges from the forest to a large lava shelf at the sea. On the right, a waterfall cascades off the rocks into the ocean. Follow the lava rock shelf to the left, reaching Queen's Bath and the ocean inlet.

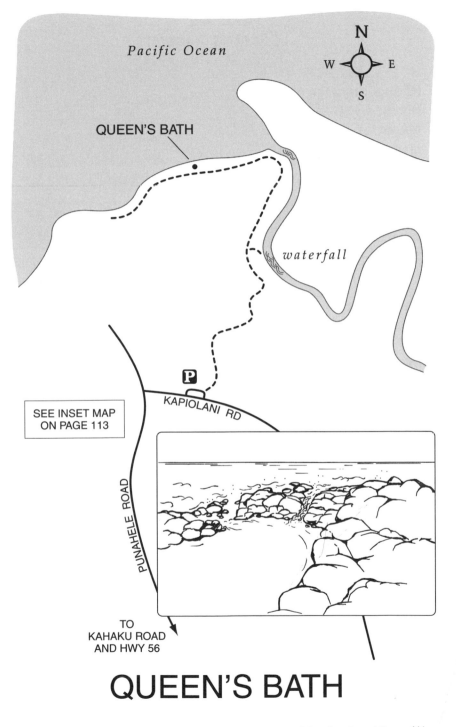

*Pacific Ocean*

N
W   E
S

QUEEN'S BATH

*waterfall*

**P**

SEE INSET MAP
ON PAGE 113

KAPIOLANI RD

PUNAHELE ROAD

TO
KAHAKU ROAD
AND HWY 56

# QUEEN'S BATH

# Hike 49
## "Hideaway's Beach"
## Pali Ke Kua Beach

**Hiking distance:** 0.6 miles round trip
**Hiking time:** 30 minutes
**Elevation gain:** 150 feet
**Maps:** U.S.G.S. Hanalei

**Summary of hike:** Hideaway's Beach (also called Pali Ke Kua) is actually two sandy beach coves separated by a lava rock point. An offshore reef stretches along the coast. These pockets of sand are nestled at the base of the steep forested cliffs in Princeville. This trail is a short and steep descent through the forest with magical views of the cliffs and coastline. The path reaches the west pocket of Hideaway's Beach beneath the Puu Poa condominiums. Access to the east beach pocket is on a paved path used by guests of the Pali Ke Kua condominiums.

**Driving directions:** From Lihue, drive 28 miles north and west on Highway 56 to Kahaku Road at the Princeville sign, just before the Princeville Shopping Center. Turn right and drive 2.1 miles to the public parking lot on the right, just before entering the Princeville Hotel.

**Hiking directions:** At the east end of the parking lot (away from the Princeville Hotel) follow the narrow, grassy corridor between two fencelines. At the edge of the bluffs, steep steps with a railing descend through the jungle. The steps end about halfway down. A steep, muddy path demanding your full concentration leads down to the secluded, pristine cove, backdropped by the lush vertical cliffs and hala and kamani trees. The second beach of Pali Ke Kua is off to the right, but it may not be accessible from the beach, depending on the tide and surf. To return, hike back up the cliffside.

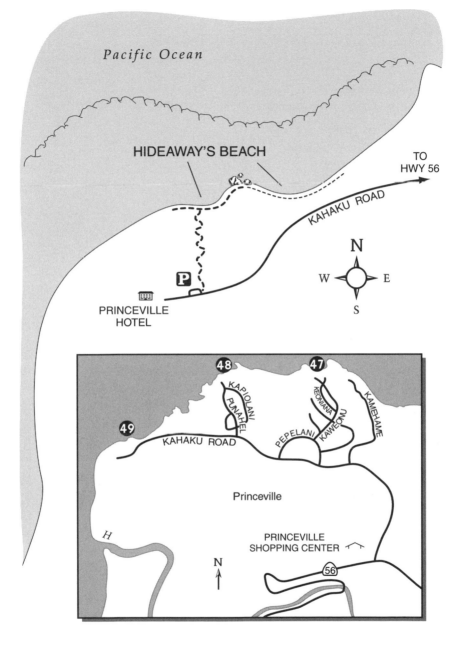

Pacific Ocean

HIDEAWAY'S BEACH

TO HWY 56

KAHAKU ROAD

N
W · E
S

P

PRINCEVILLE HOTEL

48
KAPIOLANI
PUNAHEL
47
KEONIANA
KAWEONU
KAMEHAME
49
KAHAKU ROAD
PEPELANI

Princeville

H

PRINCEVILLE SHOPPING CENTER

N

56

# HIDEAWAY'S BEACH
## (PALI KE KUA BEACH)

# Hike 50
# Hanalei River Trail
Recommended: mosquito repellent

**Hiking distance:** 3 miles round trip
**Hiking time:** 1.5 hours
**Elevation gain:** 200 feet
**Maps:** U.S.G.S. Hanalei
Northwestern Kauai Recreational Map

**Summary of hike:** This hike is a deep jungle experience in the Hanalei Valley. The trail takes you through tall bamboo forests, across streams and into deep, dense tropical vegetation with overhanging branches, roots and ferns. It leads to the Hanalei River, Kauai's largest river. White shoes are not recommended.

**Driving directions:** From Lihue, drive 30.5 miles north and west on Highway 56 towards Hanalei. Continue past Princeville. Just after crossing a long one-lane bridge over the Hanalei River, turn left on Ohiki Road. The sign at this turn reads "Hanalei National Wildlife Refuge." There are large cultivated taro fields on the right side of the road after the turn. Continue for two miles on this road, and park near the hunters' check-in booth.

**Hiking directions:** From the parking area, hike south along the rutted, muddy road through the tropical forest. At one mile the road narrows to a footpath. Watch on the left for a clearly visible trail that descends through a dense forest to the first stream crossing. Rocks can be used as stepping stones to ford the stream. Continue through the bamboo forest to a second stream crossing. A short distance after crossing, the path reaches the banks of the Hanalei River. Stroll upstream along the grassy banks of the river. Return along the same path.

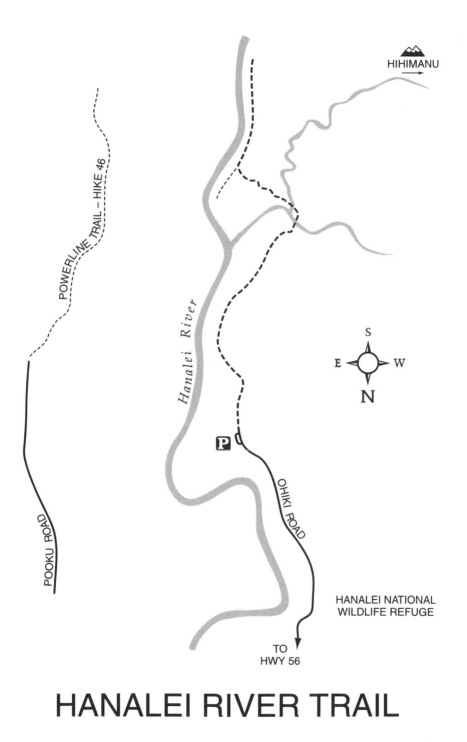

HIHIMANU

POWERLINE TRAIL – HIKE 46

*Hanalei River*

S
E ⊙ W
N

P

OHIKI ROAD

POOKU ROAD

HANALEI NATIONAL
WILDLIFE REFUGE

TO
HWY 56

# HANALEI RIVER TRAIL

# Hike 51
# Hanalei Bay
# Black Pot Beach Park to Waioli Stream

**Hiking distance:** 2.5 miles round trip
**Hiking time:** 1.5 hours
**Elevation gain:** Level
**Maps:** U.S.G.S. Hanalei

**Summary of hike:** Black Pot Beach Park sits at the mouth of the Hanalei River in picture-perfect Hanalei Bay, fringed with palms. The park, bordered by the river to the north and the Pacific to the west, has a wide, grassy camping and picnic area. Towering, fluted cliffs frame a dramatic backdrop along the arch of the semicircular bay. Several long, narrow waterfalls tumble hundreds of feet off the stately mountains. This hike follows the bay along the scenic crescent-shaped strand from the Hanalei River to Waioli Stream.

**Driving directions:** From Lihue, drive 31 miles north and west on Highway 56 to Hanalei, crossing the bridge over the Hanalei River. As you enter the town of Hanalei, turn right on Aku Road between mile markers 2 and 3. Drive 0.3 miles to Weke Road. Turn right and continue a half mile to the county park parking lot at the end of the road by the Hanalei River.

**Hiking directions:** Follow the banks of the Hanalei River across the wide grassy park, reaching the sandy beach where the river empties into the Pacific. Lush, forested hillsides border the river along its north shore. Bear left along the shoreline past the Hanalei Landing, an old pier. Follow the curve of the bay, passing the Hanalei Pavilion Beach Park picnic area at a half mile. Continue to Waioli Beach Park in a grove of ironwood trees. The trail ends at the banks of Waioli Stream at 1.25 miles.

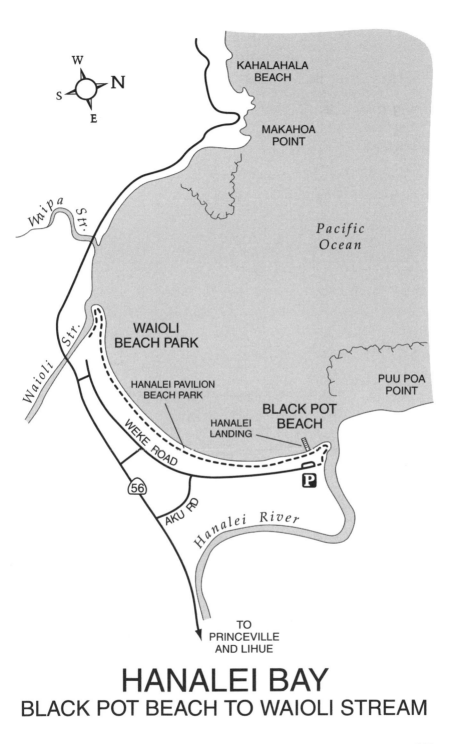

W

N

S

E

KAHALAHALA
BEACH

MAKAHOA
POINT

*Pacific
Ocean*

Waipa Str.

Waioli Str.

WAIOLI
BEACH PARK

HANALEI PAVILION
BEACH PARK

HANALEI
LANDING

BLACK POT
BEACH

PUU POA
POINT

WEKE ROAD

56

AKU RD

P

*Hanalei River*

TO
PRINCEVILLE
AND LIHUE

# HANALEI BAY
## BLACK POT BEACH TO WAIOLI STREAM

# Hike 52
# Lumahai Beach

**Hiking distance:** 1.5 miles round trip
**Hiking time:** 45 minutes
**Elevation gain:** Level
**Maps:** U.S.G.S. Hanalei

**Summary of hike:** Lumahai Beach, just west of Hanalei Bay, is a long white sand beach framed by lush vegetated cliffs. This picture-perfect location was used in the 1957 movie *South Pacific*. The Lumahai River borders the west end of the beach. Across the river, the black rock cliffs and verdant hillsides of Kolokolo Point extend out into the Pacific. To the east, views open up to Puu Poa Point at the northeast tip of Hanalei Bay. With no reef protection and powerful rip currents, swimming here is dangerous.

**Driving directions:** From Lihue, drive 34 miles north and west on Highway 56 to an unpaved beach access on the right, just shy of mile marker 6. Turn right and park in the large natural parking area under a grove of ironwood trees.

**Hiking directions:** From the parking area, go left a short distance to the mouth of the Lumahai River at the west end of the beach. Savor the views up the river and across to the huge rocky bluffs of Kolokolo Point. Return and follow the shoreline east. You may also take the forested path through the shady grove of ironwood and hau trees at the back of the beach. Both routes merge in a half mile at steep, black rock cliffs. During low tide and calm seas, you may cautiously continue around the cliffs to Kahalahala Beach, a smaller beach snuggled in a cove. The main access to Kahalahala Beach is a steep and muddy unmarked hillside trail off the shoulder of Highway 56.

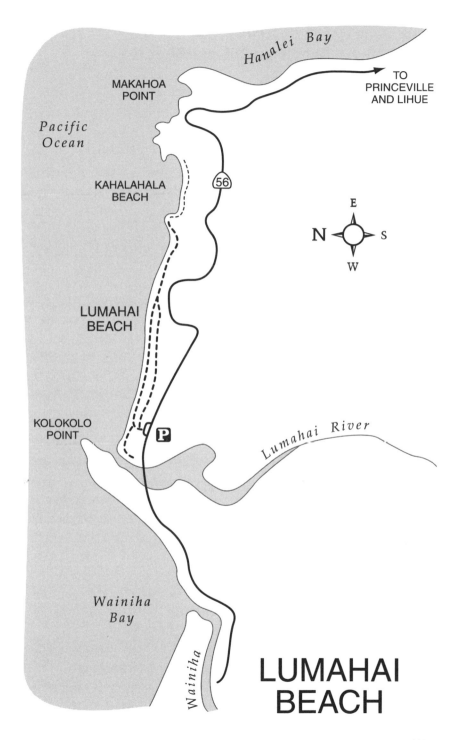

**LUMAHAI BEACH**

# Hike 53
# Kee Beach to Haena Beach Park

**Hiking distance:** 2.5 miles round trip
**Hiking time:** 1.5 hour
**Elevation gain:** Level
**Maps:** U.S.G.S. Haena

**Summary of hike:** Kee Beach borders the eastern edge of the Na Pali Cliffs in the 230-acre Haena State Park. To the east of Kee Beach is Haena Beach Park, bordered by sheer lava cliffs and the sea. The beach park has a flat, grassy camping area, sheltered picnic tables and vegetated sand dunes. A forested path with ironwood, heliotrope, kukui and almond trees connects Kee Beach with Haena Beach Park. The trail has panoramic views of the Na Pali Coast and gorgeous inland vistas of the chiseled mountain spires and green mossy cliffs.

**Driving directions:** From Lihue, drive 37 miles north and west on Highway 56 past Hanalei to the end of the road. At Princeville the mile markers begin again at 1. Park on the right side of the road at mile marker 10 in the Kee Beach parking area. Along the way, the road hugs the coast past ocean bays, caves, streams, waterfalls and crosses numerous one-lane bridges.

**Hiking directions:** Walk through the jungle setting to the beach. Two routes follow the coastline to the right (northeast). Beachcomb along the sandy shore, or follow the forested trail above the beach. Several serpentine paths interconnect, winding through the forest and along the treeline. At 0.4 miles, cross a stream and follow the narrow strand to a pile of boulders. Cross the boulders and continue on the upper forested path or sandy beach strand. Cross Limahuli Stream, reaching Haena Beach Park. Stroll through the grassy picnic and camping area. Across the road from the beach is Maniniholo Dry Cave, an ancient lava tube extending hundreds of feet underground into the mountains. Return along the same route, or follow the road back to Kee Beach, passing Waikapalae and Waikanaloa Wet Caves.

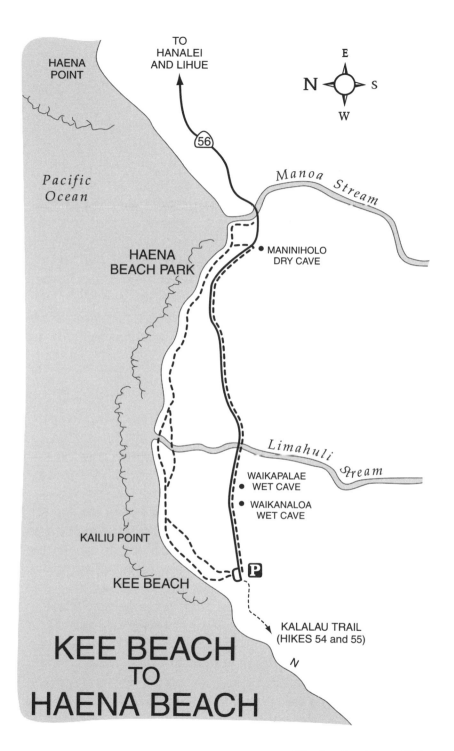

TO
HANALEI
AND LIHUE

HAENA
POINT

E

N — S

W

56

*Pacific
Ocean*

*Manoa* *Stream*

MANINIHOLO
DRY CAVE

HAENA
BEACH PARK

*Limahuli* *Stream*

WAIKAPALAE
WET CAVE

WAIKANALOA
WET CAVE

KAILIU POINT

KEE BEACH

P

KALALAU TRAIL
(HIKES 54 and 55)

N

# KEE BEACH
## TO
# HAENA BEACH

# Hike 54
## Kalalau Trail on Na Pali Coast
## Kee Beach to Hanakapiai Beach

**Hiking distance:** 4 miles round trip
**Hiking time:** 2 hours
**Elevation gain:** 1,000 feet
**Maps:** U.S.G.S. Haena

**Summary of hike:** The Kalalau Trail along the Na Pali Coast is an undeveloped, ancient Hawaiian route accessible only by foot. The 11-mile trail follows the Na Pali Coast along the edge of massive, windswept cliffs to Kalalau Beach. The rugged coastline hike overlooks a series of primeval, emerald green valleys and steep towering cliffs that drop more than 3,000 feet to the turbulent sea. This unforgettable hike covers the first two miles of the trail to Hanakapiai Beach at the mouth of Hanakapiai Valley, the first valley leading to the island's interior. To head up the valley, continue on Hike 55.

**Driving directions:** Follow driving directions for Hike 53 to Kee Beach.

**Hiking directions:** The signed trail begins on the inland side of the road by a large map and history exhibit. The uneven lava rock path, which is usually wet and at times slippery, immediately climbs through the lush tropical vegetation. In the first half mile, numerous vista points overlook Kee Beach, the scalloped Na Pali coastline and the precipitous cliffs dropping off into the fierce, pounding surf. Continue steadily uphill, traversing the cliffs for one mile. The trail levels out, and at 1.5 miles, begins to descend towards Hanakapiai Beach. Short, steep switchbacks lead down to the stream past "tsunami" warning signs. Cross Hanakapiai Stream at the white sand beach to a signed junction. This is our turnaround spot.

To hike further, the right fork climbs out of the valley and continues on the Kalalau Trail (permit required). Hike 55 follows the Hanakapiai Falls Trail to the left to a beautiful waterfall.

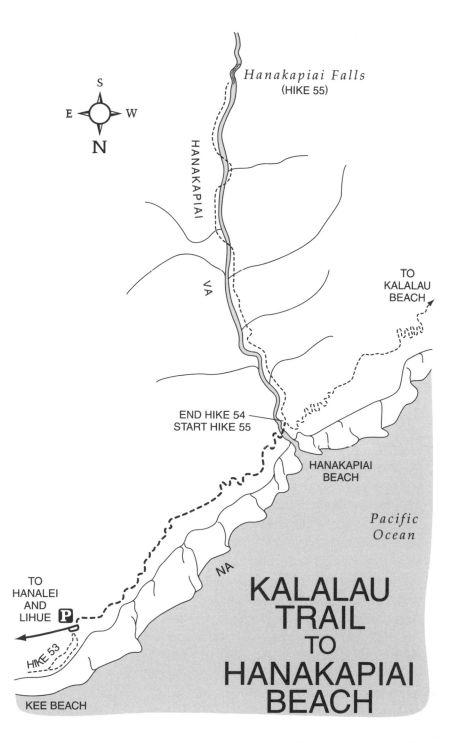

Hanakapiai Falls
(HIKE 55)

HANAKAPIAI

VA

TO
KALALAU
BEACH

END HIKE 54
START HIKE 55

HANAKAPIAI
BEACH

Pacific
Ocean

NA

TO
HANALEI
AND
LIHUE

HIKE 53

KEE BEACH

KALALAU
TRAIL
TO
HANAKAPIAI
BEACH

S
E · W
N

# Hike 55
## Kalalau Trail on Na Pali Coast
## Hanakapiai Beach to Hanakapiai Falls

**Hiking distance:** 8 miles round trip (from Kee Beach)
**Hiking time:** 5 hours
**Elevation gain:** 1,750 feet
**Maps:** U.S.G.S. Haena
        Northwestern Kauai Recreation Map

**Summary of hike:** The Hanakapiai Falls Trail begins two miles up the Kalalau Trail on the Na Pali Coast at Hanakapiai Beach— the turnaround spot for Hike 54. This side trail leads up Hanakapiai Valley, a steep-walled, stream-fed valley, to a 300-foot cataract and pool in a natural amphitheater. Along the way there are stream crossings and additional swimming pools.

**Driving directions:** From Lihue, drive 37 miles north and west on Highway 56 past Hanalei to the end of the road. At Princeville the mile markers begin again at 1. Park on the right side of the road at mile marker 10 in the Kee Beach parking area. Along the way, the road hugs the coast past ocean bays, caves, streams, waterfalls and crosses numerous one-lane bridges.

**Hiking directions:** Follow the hiking directions for Hike 54 to Hanakapiai Beach (2 miles). Take the left fork, heading inland into the sheltered Hanakapiai Valley. The first mile follows the west bank of the Hanakapiai Stream, passing huge mango trees to a sheltered picnic table. Soon the trail crosses the stream and becomes more difficult to hike due to mud, erosion and stream crossings. At 1.7 miles is a large pool and two consecutive stream crossings. Continue up the narrow valley along the east bank of the stream past several small waterfalls and pools. The trail ends at the base of Hanakapiai Falls and a pool surrounded by large boulders. Mist from the falls sprays onto the thick vegetation and moss-covered rocks. Return along the same trail.

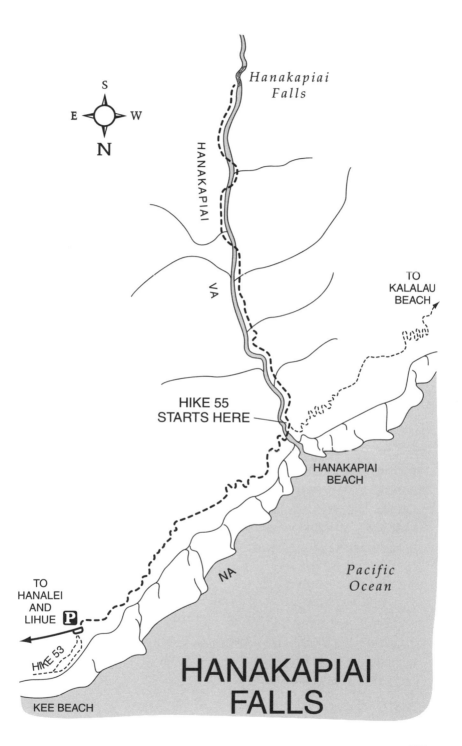

*Hanakapiai Falls*

HANAKAPIAI

VA

TO KALALAU BEACH

HIKE 55 STARTS HERE

HANAKAPIAI BEACH

NA

*Pacific Ocean*

TO HANALEI AND LIHUE

P

HIKE 53

KEE BEACH

# HANAKAPIAI FALLS

# DAY HIKE BOOKS

| | | |
|---|---|---|
| Day Hikes On the California Central Coast | 1-57342-031-X | $14.95 |
| Day Hikes On the California Southern Coast | 1-57342-045-X | 14.95 |
| Day Hikes Around Monterey and Carmel | 1-57342-036-0 | 14.95 |
| Day Hikes Around Big Sur | 1-57342-041-7 | 14.95 |
| Day Hikes In San Luis Obispo County | 1-57342-051-4 | 15.95 |
| Day Hikes Around Santa Barbara | 1-57342-042-5 | 14.95 |
| Day Hikes Around Ventura County | 1-57342-043-3 | 14.95 |
| Day Hikes Around Los Angeles | 1-57342-044-1 | 14.95 |
| Day Hikes Around Orange County | 1-57342-047-6 | 15.95 |
| Day Hikes In Yosemite National Park | 1-57342-037-9 | 11.95 |
| Day Hikes In Sequoia and Kings Canyon Nat'l. Parks | 1-57342-030-1 | 12.95 |
| Day Hikes Around Sedona, Arizona | 1-57342-049-2 | 14.95 |
| Day Hikes On Oahu | 1-57342-038-7 | 11.95 |
| Day Hikes On Maui | 1-57342-039-5 | 11.95 |
| Day Hikes On Kauai | 1-57342-040-9 | 11.95 |
| Day Hikes In Hawaii | 1-57342-050-6 | 16.95 |
| Day Hikes In Yellowstone National Park | 1-57342-048-4 | 12.95 |
| Day Hikes In Grand Teton National Park | 1-57342-046-8 | 11.95 |
| Day Hikes In the Beartooth Mountains Red Lodge, MT to Yellowstone Nat'l. Park | 1-57342-052-2 | 13.95 |
| Day Hikes Around Bozeman, Montana | 1-57342-033-6 | 11.95 |
| Day Hikes Around Missoula, Montana | 1-57342-032-8 | 11.95 |

These books may be purchased at your local bookstore or outdoor shop. Or, order them direct from the distributor:

## The Globe Pequot Press

246 Goose Lane • P.O. Box 480 • Guilford, CT 06437-0480
on the web: www.globe-pequot.com

**800-243-0495** DIRECT   **800-820-2329** FAX

DAY HIKES ON THE
California Central Coast
71 GREAT HIKES
Robert Stone

DAY HIKES ON THE
California Southern Coast
100 GREAT HIKES
Robert Stone

DAY HIKES AROUND
Monterey & Carmel
77 GREAT HIKES
Robert Stone

DAY HIKES AROUND
Big Sur
80 GREAT HIKES
Robert Stone

DAY HIKES IN
SAN LUIS OBISPO COUNTY CALIFORNIA
ROBERT STONE

DAY HIKES AROUND
Santa Barbara
82 GREAT HIKES
Robert Stone
2nd EDITION

DAY HIKES AROUND
Ventura County
82 GREAT HIKES
Robert Stone
2nd EDITION

LOS ANGELES TIMES BESTSELLER
DAY HIKES AROUND
Los Angeles
82 GREAT HIKES
Robert Stone
4th EDITION

DAY HIKES AROUND
Orange County
108 GREAT HIKES
Robert Stone

DAY HIKES IN
Yosemite
NATIONAL PARK
55 GREAT HIKES
Robert Stone
3rd EDITION

DAY HIKES IN
Sequoia & Kings Canyon
NATIONAL PARKS
Robert Stone

DAY HIKES AROUND
Sedona
ARIZONA
100 GREAT HIKES
Robert Stone
2nd EDITION

DAY HIKES ON
Oahu
57 GREAT HIKES
Robert Stone
3rd EDITION

DAY HIKES ON
Maui
55 GREAT HIKES
Robert Stone
3rd EDITION

DAY HIKES ON
Kauai
55 GREAT HIKES
Robert Stone
4th EDITION

DAY HIKES IN
Yellowstone
NATIONAL PARK
82 GREAT HIKES
Robert Stone
4th EDITION

DAY HIKES IN
Grand Teton
NATIONAL PARK
72 GREAT HIKES
Robert Stone
4th EDITION

DAY HIKES IN THE
BEARTOOTH MOUNTAINS
RED LODGE, MONTANA TO YELLOWSTONE NATIONAL PARK
ROBERT STONE

DAY HIKES AROUND
Bozeman
MONTANA
INCLUDING THE GALLATIN CANYON AND PARADISE VALLEY
Robert Stone
2nd EDITION

DAY HIKES AROUND
Missoula
MONTANA
INCLUDING THE BITTERROOTS AND THE SEELEY-SWAN VALLEY
Robert Stone
2nd EDITION

# Notes

## About the Author

Since 1991, veteran hiker Robert Stone has been writer, photographer, and publisher of Day Hike Books. Robert has hiked every trail in the *Day Hike Book* series. With 21 hiking guides in the series, many in their third and fourth editions, he has hiked thousands of miles of trails throughout the western United States and Hawaii. When Robert is not hiking, he researches, writes, and maps the hikes before returning to the trails. He is an active member of RMOWP (Rocky Mountain Outdoor Writers and Photographers), OWAC (Outdoor Writers Associaton of California), and a Los Angeles Times Best Selling Author. Robert spends summers in the Rocky Mountains of Montana and winters on the California Central Coast.